Hire a Pro

The Hiring Manager's Guide to Finding and Keeping the Best Long-term Employees

Carey Baker

Owner, Part Time Pros

Published by Expert Message Group, LLC

Expert Message Group, LLC
P.O. Box 949
Tulsa, OK 74101

415.523.0404

www.expertmessagegroup.com

First Printing, April 2012

ISBN 978-1-936875-06-1

Printed in the United States of America
Set in Arno Pro 12.5/16.5

For permissions, please contact:
Expert Message Group, LLC
P.O. Box 949
Tulsa, OK 74101

I would like to dedicate this book to my husband Brett.
Brett has continued to be my champion, and has always encouraged
me to do more than I ever thought possible. Without his encouragement
and support this book would not be a reality.

About the author

Carey Baker began Part-Time Pros with her husband Brett Baker in 2008 after having her first daughter and realizing the need for flexibility in the corporate lifestyle. Part-Time Pros staffing company unites talented professionals with companies that have full- and part-time needs. The professionals range from stay-at-home moms wanting to contribute to their household income, to the early retirees looking to supplement retirement. The Tulsa-based company, which took second place in the 2009 Mayor's Entrepreneurial Spirit Award, works with more than 400 employer contracts and more than 6000 professionals. In 2011, Part-Time Pros was one of 75 businesses in the US to receive the US Chamber Blue Ribbon Award for growth and sustainability. In her free time, Carey loves date nights with her husband Brett, cross fit, and rough housing with her girls. The Bakers live in Tulsa, Oklahoma with their two daughters Kennedy and Gentry. Carey is available to speak to your organization or association, call (918) 551-7767 for booking.

Contents

How to Use This Book

Most business owners I know don't have a lot of spare time on their hands. When they are not actually working *in* their business, they are usually working *on* their business, coming up with ways to improve, expand, and grow. Juggling their business and personal lives is a huge balancing act, leaving little time for anything but the most valued of their personal passions.

Personally, I do not have enough time to read the way I used to. I was an English major and used to love to read but now as a business owner, wife and mother time does not seem to allow for it. When I do read, it is more about researching and scanning for information I need. Whether or not you are like me in that respect, I wrote this book with that idea always in mind. I want you to be able to pick up this book and find exactly what you need to know when you need to know it.

Don't get me wrong; there is no extraneous information in these pages. Everything is pertinent to hiring and keeping good employees. However, you don't really need to read it in sequential order and cover-to-cover, though I expect by the time you look for all the information you need, you will have done just that.

If your needs one day involve placing an ad for an opening within your company, and on another day you are preparing for a performance evaluation, you can just flip to those sections.

The pages that follow will take you through the employee search process from ad to interview to evaluation. They are filled with lists and forms that I use in my own business, as well as scenarios I have encountered. You will easily find the precise information you need by referring to the index, where you will be directed to everything from lists of the very best questions to ask during an interview to sample Performance Evaluation forms to the top qualities that the best bosses possess.

The flip side is meant for the job seeker, but it can give you great insight into the challenges and perceptions of your employees, present, past and future.

Introduction

Because I've been where you are and understand all too well the challenges small business owners face daily, I'm compelled to share the knowledge I've gained while journeying the same path you're on. The reasons you began your business are probably different from the reasons I began mine or someone else began his, but we all have at least one thing in common. We want our businesses to be successful. We want them to grow.

I've learned a great deal about myself, some positive, some negative, and I know exactly where I would have done things differently. So, why wouldn't I want to share the experiences I've had and the knowledge I've acquired to help other small business owners achieve their own goals? I can't think of a single reason why not. In fact, I'd be remiss if I didn't. Creating a positive cycle of give-and-take helps small businesses, along with their owners and employees, grow and thrive.

Every person alive has the propensity to be a business owner. Owning a business may be more realistic for some than others, but it is a real possibility for anyone. That said, not everyone knows *how* to be a business owner and what the most important aspects of running a successful small business really are. Knowing your business and running your business are two very different things. There are many roles to fill, from bookkeeper to customer service rep to salesperson, and when you're lucky enough to get to the point where you stop wearing all the hats and hire people to fill those positions, that's when you need to learn two other important roles—human resources director and boss.

Most small business owners have little or no Human Resources (HR) background, though HR plays a huge role in larger corporations and exists to benefit the employer and employees. HR is instrumental in locating, interviewing, and hiring employees for larger companies. HR employees are trained in policy and procedure and in asking the right questions to determine candidates who are a good fit for the open positions within the company.

As a business owner, you must remember that you are only as good as the team you bring on—the people you hire to create the items, products, and services you are selling. Relying on someone else for your business's success is not easy. I'm not referring to your customers and clients here, though of course you need them! However, before them, you need the right person or the right team working in and for your business.

I cannot emphasize enough the importance and value—to your success and to your sanity—of finding the person who best fits your personal needs and your business's professional needs. Finding the right person rarely happens by chance. It isn't random. If you want to roll the dice and let the chips fall where they may, go to a casino. Odds are, you'll have better luck there than you will with an employee you've hired without taking the proper steps and measures.

Yes, sometimes it's trial and error. It's difficult to know beyond a doubt that a person you've met only a handful of times is the solution to your business needs. However, there are definitive processes you can follow and procedures you can implement to help you make a safe bet. Why gamble on something this important?

Your goal is to hire an employee who meets your needs and exceeds your expectations. Asking the right questions, being thorough, and providing detailed information will help you be more consistent and confident in your employee selection process. I'll take you through it, step by step, and even show you some missteps to avoid. I focus on what you need to do as a hiring professional.

Before we delve into the processes in the pages that follow, there's one other major factor for you to consider. Small business owners who take on employees find out quickly that their own role as boss is critical to how employees perform in their roles. Part of the process, then, is to examine your own management style and the work atmosphere you are providing. If you want to attract good employees, you need to be a good boss. If you want employees to remain with your company, you need to provide a positive, productive work atmosphere. There are plenty of simple things you can do to accomplish both.

In the long run, putting in the time and effort and maybe a little bit of cash at the front end will result in a win-win situation for your company and your employees.

SECTION 1
The Hiring Process

The moment you're ready to begin hiring help in your business, I strongly encourage you not to. At least, not right away. Don't rush online and place that ad on Craigslist too quickly. Before you can even think about taking on an employee, you need to know a couple of things about yourself and your business.

Step 1: Determine the position and budget

Ask yourself these two questions first:

1. What can I afford?

2. What is it that I am looking for?

The answers will help you **determine the job position and your budget** for that position. When I started my company, for example, I knew after a very short period I needed administrative help. I determined I could afford to hire someone for 20 hours per week at a rate of $12 per hour. Now that I knew that, I could place an ad for admin help, right? Not yet. If I had, here's what my job description would have read:

- Admin Help wanted

- 20 hours per week

- $12 per hour

That doesn't even scratch the surface of the work I need done, nor does it tell potential applicants a thing about the work they would be expected to do. Truthfully, a job description like the one above is simply a huge waste of everyone's time. All it does is create more work—for the hiring employer and for the applicant.

The hiring employer will receive a barrage of resumes and applications from individuals who think they might be a good fit, and then spend hours of valuable time going through the stack to find the one or two who actually are, or worse, pass over a qualified person by accident. Why not take the time to determine the qualifications needed for the position first and reduce the likelihood of unqualified applicants? Posting an ambiguous job description is also a disservice to the job seeker who takes the time to apply without really knowing what skills you're looking for.

Step 2: The job description

So, although I have established a budget and a job position, I need to create a job description of the thing that I need help with. A detailed job description is so critical and so valuable, on so many levels, for so many reasons. Writing one will take up a good many of the already scant hours in your day but will save you time, money and aggravation down the road. A detailed job description will protect you in the end. Trust me.

Once you have defined your own budget, step back and create a good job description that embodies most, if not all, of what an employee will need to do in the role you want filled. You may discover that you can't afford the number of hours it will require for an employee to perform all the job requirements you establish. You may need to do some tweaking and restructuring to meet your budget; or you may discover you can add more tasks to fill the hours you allot for the job.

The detailed job description you create will help you focus on the skills you need a potential employee to have to be considered for the job. Your job description can then serve as a checklist of the minimum criteria an applicant needs to meet. The more familiar and knowledgeable you are about the requirements an applicant needs to meet for an open position, the more adept you will be at scanning résumés to determine whether the applicants have the skills and experience you need.

The job description will also be a useful tool after an applicant has been hired, as it will clearly detail what you expect from the person you've hired. We'll get into this more later on, when we discuss tracking and performance evaluation.

When you've determined everything you need in an employee and the skills he or she needs to do the work you require, you will be able to create a thorough job description, like the one below, which will help you create an informative job advertisement that will attract only qualified applicants.

EXECUTIVE ADMINISTRATIVE ASSISTANT

Job Description

- Reports to: President

- Salary: $20.00/hour

- Position Type: Full-time non-exempt (exempt employees must meet the U.S. Department of Labor criteria. Please refer to these criteria. If the job does not meet the requirements, the position will be non-exempt.)

JOB SUMMARY

Local company is seeking a full-time executive administrative assistant to work in a corporate office. The professional hired will provide administrative assistance to the President of the company. The person hired will work with minimal instruction or supervision.

ESSENTIAL FUNCTIONS

- Drafts correspondence, memoranda, etc., for internal and/or external distribution.

- Coordinates all travel for the President.

- May prepare agendas and materials related thereto, and see that all legal requirements are met.

- Conserves the President's time by reading, researching, and routing correspondence.

- Responsible for establishing and maintaining official documents and records in appropriate files.

- May be asked to attend some meetings, seminars, etc., possibly to take notes or furnish information.

- May do research for a project.

- Maintains office supplies inventory by checking stock to determine inventory level, anticipating needed supplies, evaluating new office products, placing and expediting orders for supplies, verifying receipt of supplies.

- May receive visits or calls regarding complaints that may be resolved or referred to the proper person for resolution.

- Provides coverage for other assistants when/if needed.

- Cleans out e-mail and corresponds on behalf of the President.

- Takes dictation.

- Runs personal errands for the President when needed.

- Keeps accurate and organized calendars and assists the President in preparing for meetings.

- Performs any necessary follow-up for the President after meetings.

- Performs such other duties as may be assigned.

KNOWLEDGE, SKILLS, AND ABILITIES

- Thorough knowledge of modern office practices and procedures and the use of computers, office machines, and equipment.

- Ability to understand and interpret pertinent policies and procedures clearly and accurately.

- Ability to establish and maintain effective working relationships with supervising personnel, coworkers, subordinates, the media, representatives from all levels of government, civic organizations, business professionals, and the public.

- Ability to project a positive, concerned image to the public.

- Ability to communicate effectively orally and in writing.

- Sufficient skill in typing and the ability to take sufficient notes at a meeting to prepare an accurate record of events.

- Excellent organizational skills.

- Better-than-average attendance.

TRAINING AND EXPERIENCE

- Advanced training in typing and general office procedures.

- 5+ years experience performing administrative duties.

- Bachelor's degree.

- Proficient in Microsoft Office Suite—Outlook, PowerPoint, Excel, Publisher, and Word.

COMPANY CONFORMANCE STATEMENT

In performing the respective tasks and duties, the employee hired will be expected to conform to the following:

- Perform quality work before deadlines with or without supervision.

- Interact professionally with other employees, customers, and suppliers.

- Work effectively as a team contributor on all assignments.

- Work independently while understanding the need for communicating and coordinating work efforts with other employees and organizations.

PHYSICAL REQUIREMENTS

Physical requirements for positions include arm and hand steadiness and finger dexterity enough to use a keyboard and telephone; occasional lifting up to 25 pounds; may be subject to walking, standing, sitting, and reaching; and vision, speech, and hearing sufficient to perform the essential tasks. Any physical restrictions should be discussed or noted during the interview process.

Step 3: The search process

Now that you've defined your budget and created your job description, you can begin the **search process**. This process varies from one company to another. The search for qualified applicants takes on many forms, from investing in print and online advertising to outsourcing to a staffing company, conducting a social media campaign, and/or networking with friends. Consider all the outlets at your disposal to determine where you might find the best person to fill your need. Now that you have a solid job description to share with others, they will be able to recommend people who might be a good fit. Think about how difficult it would be to find qualified candidates based on a vague explanation of duties, like the example we used for admin help.

Choose where you search for new hires wisely. If you're looking for someone to do office assistant–type tasks, you probably don't want to place your ad with a company serving specialized or high-ranking professional job seekers. Referrals from family, friends and acquaintances may appear to be a good way of filling your open position, but I caution you to assess personal recommendations as thoroughly as you would an applicant you received through an ad you posted. Just because someone you know knows someone else who is looking for a job doesn't necessarily mean that person is a good fit for your job or your company.

Once you have identified where to find potential applicants for your position, it's a matter of knowing the standards you want individuals to meet, the qualifications you want them to have, and the steps you want an interested individual to go through to move forward in the application process. How do you want applicants to apply for your job? What procedures must they follow and what purpose do those procedures serve? Do you want applicants to submit a résumé? A cover letter? Complete an online application? Call?

In my company we have every applicant complete an online application. My primary driving force for doing this goes beyond just capturing the applicant's information. Although some may think an online application is impersonal, it can be a good indicator of a person's skills and ability. For me, applying online is a key test for determining an applicant's capacity to navigate a computer and the Internet. Think of it as a way to weed out those who don't have a working knowledge of technology, or don't have adequate typing skills, or aren't conscientious enough. How can you tell that from a simple online application? If you receive an application with typos in it, for example, that is very telling of the individual's attention to detail. Everyone makes mistakes, but if an applicant is not going to check for accuracy and make sure the application is error-free, how do you think he or she will perform in the available job?

The same holds true for résumés. If you place an ad for a position, be prepared to be inundated with the skills and experiences, work histories, and academic backgrounds of hundreds of diligent job seekers, all trying to highlight their assets and capture your attention. Although résumés certainly serve a valuable purpose, reading a single resume—let alone dozens or hundreds—can be dizzying. There are a few things you can do to be prepared for the résumés review:

- First, you must know your company standards and its mission, and know the qualifications employees need to have to do their specific jobs, to know what to look for in a résumé. For example, if the tenure for a receptionist is about a year, you don't need to set a standard of five years or more of previous experience for the job.

- Just because an applicant has a job gap for the past year and a half does not mean he or she isn't a highly qualified candidate. It could be the individual has had three different job offers he or she did not accept because the individual knew the jobs were short-term solutions and not the best fit. In cases like this, the individual is not taking advantage of unemployment benefits, but being respectful to the hiring companies. Transparency is so important. If the applicant has the skills you're looking for, but hasn't worked in a while, ask about the job gap before disregarding his or her application.

- You should be able to scan résumé quickly to see if they contain the basics you need. Reading each one top to bottom is not a good use of your time. An applicant's résumé is a reflection of the individual and should present his or her skills efficiently and effectively. If a résumé is too difficult to understand, it's like trying to read a book you're not interested in. It's not going to happen.

- Once you have whittled down the résumés to only those that meet your predetermined standards and qualifications, scan the remaining ones for work history, specifics about work performance, typos, inconsistencies, or anything else that is a red flag for you.

Step 4: Interviewing candidates

Once you know what you can afford, what you need done, and where to look for qualified candidates, you need to develop a set of **interviewing questions** that will help you determine the best employee for the job.

Before I conduct person-to-person interviews, I arrange a brief five- to ten-minute preliminary interview via phone or e-mail with all those who have made it through the first cut. Here are a few examples of questions I ask (remember to tailor these to your own needs and to the specifics of the job):

1. The position will (insert your needs). Does this fit your long-term needs, or are you looking for full-time employment but will take part-time until you find full-time?

2. The position is an entry-level position. Please tell me why you would be interested in this given your experience. I want to know why I should not deem you "overqualified."

3. The position will start at $12/hour. I realize this is low pay, but I am a start-up so I have to start salaries low to determine whether there is a ROI. Please talk to me about your pay expectations and if this pay would be acceptable based on your needs.

4. What would I gain by hiring you?

5. I am looking for a right-hand gal or guy to truly be an extension of me. Tell me about how you could do this well and how you would keep me organized or help me grow my business.

6. Lets go through your work history and discuss your reasons for leaving each employer.

7. What are your long-term career goals and aspirations?

It's so important that you maintain consistency with your interviews by asking all applicants the same standard questions. This is key to making your final decision.

Without consistency, there is no true way to compare one applicant to another. If you ask different questions of applicants and then try to weigh one person's skills versus another's, there's no solid way to measure them. There's no way to compare apples to apples if you're not asking the same questions. Don't make the process more difficult than it needs to be. In addition, pre-written questions will help you interview. I often get feedback from candidates who are sent out to interview with our clients similar to the following: "Well, I don't know how the interview went; the owner did most of the talking." Small business owners in particular are so used to promoting and selling their business that they go into an interview thinking they need to sell the person on their business. Don't do this! Eighty percent of talking should come from person being interviewed with 20 percent coming from the interviewer.

When you develop your set of Face to Face interview questions, ask some that are open-ended enough to give you a sense of who the person is. Some of my favorites that should really give you insight into your applicant are the following:

1. Tell me about yourself.

2. Talk to me about your strengths.

3. Talk to me about your weaknesses.

4. Tell me about a challenging situation you experienced in a past position and how you dealt with it.

5. Walk me through a typical day at ABC Company.

6. What do you know about this company?

7. What do you know about the position we are hiring for?

8. Talk to me about what you feel you are going to bring to the table.

You also want to make sure you ask questions that speak directly to the job description you are hiring for.

1. Can you give me an example of similar projects you have led or tackled and tell me what the outcome was?

2. Tell me about your expertise performing these various functions. (Your job description will tell you what functions you need to know about: data entry, bookkeeping, scheduling, spreadsheet development, PowerPoint presentations, etc.)

You'll notice that the majority of these sample questions can be asked of applicants applying for any position. So, in addition to these examples, you want to customize at least three questions that are pertinent to the specifics of your particular job.

Sometimes, you need an icebreaker, or you get tired of asking the same questions in the same way, or you want a bit more insight into an applicant who seems to have the skills you need. Here are some of my favorite questions to accomplish that. They are great to keep in your Interview Folder. You can find and print them from my website, www.parttimepros.com.

Seven Interview Questions You Must Ask to Hire Someone Brilliant

1. How about those Sooners?
(not really, but a question to develop rapport to get the interview started)

    a. How were you affected by the 12 inches of snow we got?
    b. Are you from Tulsa?

2. Talk about a time when you had to overcome major obstacles.
(to get a picture of the person's past performance)

    a. Describe a time when you hired or fired the wrong person.
    b. What was one of the toughest problems you ever solved? What process did you go through to solve it?

3. What interests you about this position?
(to find out how the applicant feels about the position and the company)

    a. Where does this job fit into your career path?
    b. If you had to persuade a friend to apply for this job, what would you tell him or her?

4. Is there intelligent life in outer space?
(not really, but a question to find out what kind of thinker the person is and how he or she handles surprises)

    a. Teach me how to do something I don't know how to do.
    b. Why do people climb mountains?

5. Imagine we have just hired you. What's the most important thing on your to-do list on the first day of work?
(to help ascertain someone's judgment and decision-making skills; you want to see whether he or she demonstrates the competencies and priorities that are important to the job and your company)

    a. Would you tell your boss if a coworker tells you that he or she did something wrong that affects the company?

    b. How would you handle an employee whose performance is mediocre but who you know has the potential to do better?

6. Why did you get into this line of work?
(to measure the candidate's values and whether they are a fit for your company's culture; you should be looking for someone whose work ethic, motivations, and methods match those of the company)

    a. When did you realize this would be your career?

    b. What keeps you coming to work besides the paycheck?

7. But enough about you, what about us?
(to find out whether the candidate has done his or her homework)

    a. Where do you think the company should be in ten years?

    b. What is your opinion of our products or services?

Be sure to keep your questions centered on skills, experience, and past work history, though. There are questions that you should **not** ask of an employee during an interview. Some can get you in real trouble.

- Do not ask about a potential employee's religious preferences.

- Do not ask how many children an applicant has or if he or she is married.

- Do not ask if the applicant has childcare in place or what he or she will do when a child gets ill.

- Stay away from questions that refer to protected classes. Protected classes include the following:

    - Race, Color, Gender, Religious Belief, National Origin, Disability, Age, Familial Status.

    - Sexual Orientation, Veteran Status, Generic Information.

I was recently in a meeting with a client representing a company that described itself as a Christian company. He asked if I could screen only Christians. I stated that I could not, but asked him to explain the company's culture in greater detail. Did the employees pray together at the office? Did they have work bible studies? I was curious. Once I learned more about what the employees did, I relayed this information to my recruiter who was then able to communicate it to our applicants. Anyone who would not feel comfortable in this type of environment should know up front.

So, although you cannot discriminate, you can, in an interview, explain your culture and ask if the applicant would be comfortable in that type of environment.

The Interview Process Goes Both Ways

On the flip side, there are questions that *you* should be prepared to answer and information you should be able to readily give to applicants interviewing for a job with your company. Being able to tell an individual the type of work environment you offer will help him or her determine if it's the right culture. And figuring out the work culture of your company will help you understand what you need in an employee.

Not everyone will fit in every type of environment. I'm all for diversity and inclusion, but knowing who will blend with your team is so important to the production level of your business.

Hiring a suit-and-tie candidate for a window-tinting company based in a dusty garage is probably like trying to fit a square peg in a round hole.

Be able to tell applicants what your company values are so that applicants have a sense of the things that are important to you. In my own company, balance is one of our core values. I absolutely promote a healthy work/life balance for my employees and for myself. Some of the questions I ask an applicant are the following: "How do you balance your time?" "How do you fill your cup back up?" "Where do you find your peace, serenity, and happiness?" I ask these questions because I need employees who are high energy and positive; if they're not effectively balancing their lives, they are going to come to work tired and stressed out.

As an employer, you should be able to convey a sense of how things are done in your company. Is it a slower-paced, laid-back environment, or does there always seem to be a sense of urgency? Is the work structure hierarchical (my job and your job), or does everyone pitch in as needed? Can employees come to you directly with thoughts and ideas, or do they need to follow a certain protocol? Details about work schedules, dress code, training and even employee interaction should all be disclosed at the interview. Even if the applicant doesn't ask, it's a good idea to mention some of these things, as they will give the potential employee a good idea of what it's like to work there and if it's really the place for him or her.

Step 5: Analyzing your results

Once you've gone through your applications and interviewed every applicant who has met at least the minimum criteria, you must begin **analyzing** each one.

Ask yourself questions such as the following:

- Who are the individuals who have applied for this position?
- Who has the strongest skills for the position?
- Who made the best impression during their interviews?
- Who will mesh the best with my team?

Analyzing your prospects is probably one of the toughest steps in the hiring process. Ultimately, you are trying to determine which one is the best fit for your organization. Remember, you're not going into this step of the process blindly. If you've done the necessary preparation, analyzing may be difficult, but not impossible.

While you're weighing your applicants, I again caution you not to feel rushed into filling a vacant position. If you don't feel quite right, if you're not overwhelmed by a candidate, or you feel you may be making concessions just to get the position filled, chances are this person won't be a long-term hire. Bring on a temp or delegate various aspects of the unfilled position to other staff, and even yourself, until you find the applicant who is the right fit. You don't want to have to go through the same process again a few months later, so make sure you feel confident about your decision.

Remember, the whole point is to take the time and follow the steps that will help you find the right employee for the individual role you want him or her to play in your company.

Step 6: Checking references

Once you've made your hiring decision, but before you offer the position to your new employee, you absolutely must **check references**. You may already have a list of references if that was part of your application. If that wasn't one of your criteria up front, contact the potential employee and let him or her know you are collecting references for the next phase of your hiring process.

Checking in with previous employers will help you get a sense of how the employee worked, how the employee was to work with, and how the employee worked as a team member. Most hiring professionals assume that if a person is listed as a reference, the result will be a glowing review. And 80 percent of the time, that's true. However, that leaves 20 percent, in which other information can surface that can help you determine if this individual really is a good match for your organization.

Be sure to ask about the employee's specific skills and job duties in his or her past role. For example, if the résumé lists "proficient in Word, Excel, and

PowerPoint," ask the reference about the type of projects, documents, and programs the employee worked with. This will ensure that the employee actually has the tangible experience he or she professes to have.

Here's an absolutely shocking statistic to contemplate:

Seventy-three percent of applications contain false or embellished information.

That means that three-quarters of every application you receive for a job contains some inaccurate information! At least to some degree.

This is why it's essential you go the extra step to find out a little bit more about what the applicant is all about, who he or she is, and what skills he or she is really bringing to your company. And, in this day and age, if social media is not something you're looking at to assess whether someone is really the best fit for your company, why on earth not? It can really be a window into an individual. One peek at a person's Facebook page can reveal so much. If you see an employee blasting an employer through posts on Facebook, that should give you pause about whether this is the type of person you want to bring on. I recently wanted to hire an additional staff member. He interviewed well, his references were good, he passed the background check and drug screen, and then I decided to do one last check of his social media presence. I came upon two older LinkedIn profiles. One listed an employer that was nowhere on his résumé and had not come up during his interview. I had friends who worked there at the time, and I reached out to them. Through my research, I learned that he had been terminated because of some very unethical behavior. I was glad I did the research. He falsified his application, which was his first mistake, and his termination made me question his integrity. Do your part to make sure you hire the right person!

When you speak to a professional reference, also ask for the employee's specific job title. Applicants sometimes misrepresent their true position, either bumping up their title to reflect a higher-level position or downgrading their title to avoid appearing overqualified.

One of my clients wanted to alter his title of Vice President of Operations to Executive Administrative Assistant, because he felt companies were not considering him for positions due to his higher level of experience. Naturally, we strongly discouraged that, as this misrepresentation would reflect negatively on him if a company performed a reference check and discovered he wasn't being honest. Although his skills would not be questioned, his tactics and integrity might be.

As a small business owner, you must do your due diligence: check with past employers and speak to other references before making a new hire. Be sure you cover the basic questions:

1. What was the employee's title at your company?

2. Did the employee work for you, with you, or as your supervisor/manager?

3. What type of work/projects did the employee do?

4. What computer programs did the employee use to accomplish the job?

5. Did the employee work as part of a team?

If necessary, bring on a background screening company if you see or sense behaviors that really aren't going to complement your organization or its culture.

As a potential employer, you are entitled to ask references certain questions, but you should steer clear of certain areas. You always want to talk with past employers about the applicant's skills and experience. Avoid any conversations that go down the personality path. Even though personality does affect your company and the team, you need to start with skills. However, you can ask questions in ways that will give you a sense of the person behind the skills.

1. Talk to me about this individual's role in your company.

2. Can you tell me about his or her strengths? What was he/she good at?

3. Can you tell me about any weaknesses?

4. How did this individual handle his or her weaknesses?

5. Was this individual ever counseled on his or her weaknesses?

6. How did he or she take that feedback? Did he or she embrace it? Was
    he or she resistant? Defensive?

All of these questions focus on skills but can give you a good sense
of how someone handles certain situations and enable you, as a hiring
professional, to ascertain if the candidate will fit into your job culture.

When you speak with previous employers, you should expect and
are entitled to honesty and disclosure. It is their duty to pass along any
information about negative things that happened that were the employee's
responsibility. Laws protect previous employers by allowing them to share
negative information, such as embezzlement or sexual harassment, without
fear of repercussion, because the information will have a positive impact
on the interviewing company's future. For example, a former employer is
allowed to disclose that the individual applying for an accounting position
at your company embezzled funds.

There are ways you can ask questions tailored to these situations:

1. Was there anything this individual did that was unethical or illegal in
    his or her role with your company?

2. Was there ever a situation in which you questioned the individual's
    integrity?

Step 7: Making an offer

Once you've made your final hiring decision, it's time to formally offer
the position to your new employee, contingent on a clear background check
and drug screening, if that's part of your process.

Your **offer letter** should mirror the job description you created way
back in the beginning of this process. Really, if you take the time to do
that first step and create a good, solid job description, you can just copy
and paste that into the offer letter. Your offer letter doesn't need to be
complex and should display your enthusiasm about the employee joining
your company. The letter should contain detailed information about hours,

pay, and everything pertinent to your agreement with the employee. The offer letter should also contain any pertinent legal information such as non-competes, confidentiality clauses, etc.

Following is an example of the offer letter I used when I hired my executive administrative assistant. You will notice that it contains all of the details from the job description.

Date

Offer Letter

Employee Name
Employee Address

Dear _____:

On behalf of Part-Time Pros, I am pleased to offer you a position as the Executive Administrative Assistant. This position will report to the CEO, Carey Baker. In Carey's absence, you should direct all questions to the COO, Brett Baker. We would like to offer you the position with starting compensation of $20.00/hour. You will be needed approximately 40 hours a week. You will be paid biweekly. This position is considered a non-exempt position for purposes of federal wage-hour law, which means that you will be eligible for overtime pay for hours actually worked in excess of 40 in a given workweek.

The expected office hours will be 8:00–5:00 p.m. Monday through Friday with an hour to take each day for lunch.

In addition to your compensation, you will be eligible to receive the benefits offered to all Part-Time Pros employees. These benefits are described in the enclosed materials. We also have enclosed a copy of the employee handbook, which describes the company's policies and procedures that will govern certain aspects of your employment. Please be sure to review the handbook and sign and return the acknowledgment of receipt page at the end of the handbook. You will receive all company-paid holidays and be entitled to seven paid vacation days and five paid sick days. Paid Time Off (PTO) will be initially accrued at xx hours per month; however, PTO is available for use only after three consecutive months of employment. Accrual of PTO is retroactive to your actual start date.

Eligibility for health and dental coverage, a 401(k) pension plan, and flexible spending accounts is subject to plan terms.

Eligibility for company-paid benefits such as life insurance, short- and long-term disability, and long-term care, is subject to applicable waiting periods.

Basic job duties and company expectations are, but not limited to, the following:

- Drafts correspondence, memoranda, etc., for internal and/or external distribution.

- Coordinates all travel for the President.

- May prepare agendas and materials related thereto, and see that all legal requirements are met.

- Conserves the President's time by reading, researching, and routing correspondence.

- Responsible for establishing and maintaining official documents and records in appropriate files.

- May be asked to attend some meetings, seminars, etc., possibly to take notes or furnish information.

- May do research for a project.

- Maintains office supplies inventory by checking stock to

determine inventory level, anticipating needed supplies, evaluating new office products, placing and expediting orders for supplies, verifying receipt of supplies.

- May receive visits or calls regarding complaints that may be resolved or referred to the proper person for resolution.

- Provides coverage for other assistants when/if needed.

- Cleans out e-mail and corresponds on behalf of the President.

- Takes dictation.

- Runs personal errands for the President when needed.

- Keeps accurate and organized calendars and assists the President in preparing for meetings.

- Performs any necessary follow-up for the President after meetings.

- Has thorough knowledge of modern office practices and procedures and the use of computers, office machines, and equipment.

- Can understand and interpret pertinent policies and procedures clearly and accurately.

- Can establish and maintain effective working relationships with supervising personnel, coworkers, subordinates, the media, representatives from all levels of government, civic organizations, business professionals, and the public.

- Can project a positive, concerned image to the public.

- Can communicate effectively orally and in writing.

- Has sufficient skill in typing and can take sufficient notes at a meeting to prepare an accurate record of events.

- Has excellent organizational skills.

- Has better-than-average attendance.

- Assists the team and performs such other duties as may be assigned.

  Performance Development Plan and salary review will occur at six months of employment and then 12 months of employment if reached.

Amendments/Modifications/ Miscellaneous

The provisions contained herein may be amended, modified, or rescinded in whole or in part, at any time by Part-Time Pros at its sole discretion. The provisions of this document are intended to replace any earlier documents and memoranda concerning payment structure. Nothing contained in this document or any other company document is intended to alter the at-will nature of any employee's employment.

Terms of Employment

In consideration of my employment by Part-Time Pros ("Company"), I agree as follows:

1. **Confidential Information.**

(a) **Definition.** "Confidential Information" means the proprietary information and trade secrets of Company and its customers as described below:

(i) Included in "Confidential Information" are the object code and source code to Company's software, Company's marketing plans and strategies, Company's plans for new product development, Company's technical designs, Company's data dictionaries, information relating to Company's financial status, and any other information that Company marks confidential or by separate memorandum or e-mail informs me is confidential.

(ii) Also included in "Confidential Information" is any information about Company's customers that I have access to in performing my employment duties for Company.

(iii) Excluded from "Confidential Information" is information that: (x) I can prove was in my possession before I received it from the Company, (y) is in the public domain through no fault of my own, or (z) I learned from a third party not related to Company. Information licensed by Company to customers under a confidentiality restriction is not considered to be in the public domain.

(b) **Nondisclosure.** I agree that I will not disclose Confidential Information to any third party not employed by Company unless Company authorizes me to do so in writing. I further agree that I will not use Confidential Information for any purpose except to perform my employment duties for Company. These agreements will continue to apply after I am no longer employed by Company.

2. **Return of Company Property.** Upon termination of my employment with Company, I will promptly deliver to Company, without copying or summarizing, all material related to Company's business that is in my possession or under my control, including, without limitation, all physical property, keys, documents, lists, electronic information storage media, manuals, letters, notes, and reports.

3. **Works Made For Hire.** I understand that any work that I create or help create at the request of Company, including software, user manuals, training materials, sales materials, and other written and visual works, are works made for hire to which Company owns the copyright. I may not reproduce or publish these copyrighted works, except in the pursuit of my employment duties.

4. **Inventions.** Any inventions, discoveries, and ideas ("Technology") that I develop while performing work assigned to me by Company are owned by Company. I will sign any assignment or other document requested by Company to establish Company's ownership of the Technology and to permit Company to obtain and retain patents, copyrights, trademarks, and other indication of ownership, without charge to Company, but at no expense to me. If there is Technology that I developed before becoming employed by Company and to which I claim ownership, I have listed it here: _____.

5. **Prior Agreements.** I have provided Company copies of all agreements with previous employers under which I have agreed not to compete or otherwise agreed to limit the use of trade secrets.

6. **Full-Time Employment.** While I am employed by Company, I will devote my full-time best efforts to Company's business and will not engage in any other business or employment without the prior written approval of Company's President.

7. **Post-Employment Restriction.**

(a) **Definition.** "Competitive Products" means a product or service sold by Company or competitive with a product or service sold by Company while I am an employee of Company.

(b) **Non-Compete Agreement.** During the time I am employed by Company and for a period of two years after my employment with Company terminates, I will not, without the prior written consent of Company:

(i) Design, develop, sell, manufacture, license, distribute, or solicit orders for Competitive Products.(ii) Affiliate as an owner, officer, director, member, manager, employee, or agent with any business enterprise that designs, develops, sells, manufactures, distributes, licenses, or solicits orders for a Competitive Product. (iii) Solicit any customer or employee of Company to discontinue the customer or employee relationship with Company.

I ACKNOWLEDGE THAT THE FOREGOING RESTRICTIONS ARE REASONABLE AND APPROPRIATE MEANS OF PROTECTING COMPANY'S PROPER INTERESTS, WHICH WILL NOT UNREASONABLY INTERFERE WITH MY ABILITY TO MAKE A LIVING.

8. **Injunctive Relief.** I recognize that if I breach this Agreement, Company's business will suffer irreparable harm and that remedies at law will be inadequate. I agree that in the case of any breach or threatened breach of this Agreement, Company is entitled to immediate injunctive relief or a decree of specific performance of this Agreement, in addition to any other remedies provided by law and without being required to prove irreparable harm or special damages.

9. **Entire Agreement; Modifications.** This Agreement is my entire agreement with Company with respect to its subject matter and supersedes any prior written or oral understandings pertaining thereto. My obligations under this Agreement may not be changed in whole or in part except by a written agreement

signed by the President of Company and me and specifically refers to this Agreement.

10. **Binding Effect.** This Agreement may be assigned by Company in connection with any transfer or sale of its business, and shall inure to the benefit of Company and its successors and assigns. This Agreement is binding upon me, my heirs, personal representatives, successors, and assigns.

11. **Severability.** I agree that the provisions of this Agreement are fair and reasonable in light of my employment relationship with Company and the nature of Company's business. Nevertheless, if a court of competent jurisdiction should invalidate any provision of this Agreement, all other provisions shall survive and remain valid and enforceable. If a court of competent jurisdiction should decline to enforce any provision on the ground that it is over-broad or unreasonable, that provision shall be narrowed only to the extent required so that it may be enforceable under State law.

12. **Captions.** Any captions and headings are purely for the convenience of the reader and shall not be used to interpret or construe this Agreement.

13. **Governing Law.** The interpretation of this Agreement and the obligations hereunder are governed by the laws of the State.

Your start date is scheduled for xxxx. On your first day, you will be given an orientation by Human Resources at 8:00 a.m., which will include completing employment forms, reviewing fringe benefits, and touring the premises. Please bring appropriate documentation to complete your new hire forms, including proof that you are presently eligible to work in the United States for I-9 purposes. Failure to provide appropriate documentation within three days of hire will result in immediate termination of employment in accordance with the terms of the Immigration Reform and Control Act. If you need information regarding which documents to bring, please feel free to contact me. You will also need to review and sign the Part-Time Pros employee policy manual and return the acknowledgment of receipt page at the end of the handbook to me. We greatly look forward to having you join Part-Time Pros and become a member of our team. However, we recognize that you retain the option, as does Part-Time Pros, of ending your employment with Part-Time Pros at any time, with or without notice and with or without cause. Thus, your employment with Part-Time Pros is at-will, and neither this letter nor any other oral or written representations may be considered a contract for any specific period of time.

We look forward to you joining our team of professionals and helping us continue to build a strong, growing, and profitable organization.

If you wish to accept the offer, please sign in the place provided below and return it to me.

I am pleased to be able to extend this offer to you and look forward to your formal acceptance. Should you have any questions about starting with Part-Time Pros, please do not hesitate to contact me.

Sincerely,

Carey Dunkin Baker

_____

The provisions of this offer of employment have been read and are understood, and the offer is herewith accepted. I understand that my employment is contingent upon [completion of background check, drug test, execution of an employment agreement, or any other contingencies outlined above].

This offer shall remain open until xxxxx. Any acceptance postmarked after this date will be considered invalid.

Date: _____

Signature: _____

Reporting Date: _____

These SEVEN STEPS are the critical, initial steps that will help you do the very best job possible in hiring the right person for your company. While I explained the process in detail throughout the pages of this chapter, it's really not all that complicated and can be summed up right here:

1. Define your budget

2. Create your job description

3. Determine your search process

4. Develop your interview questions

5. Analyze candidates

6. Check references

7. Extend formal offer

Basically, it's just a matter of asking:

WHO

- Who are you considering to fill the position?
- Who do you need to talk to to finalize your decision?

WHAT

- What can you pay?
- What do you need?
- What questions will you ask applicants?

WHEN

- When do you want to make an offer and have your new hire begin?

WHERE

- Where will you search to find the best possible employee?

SECTION 2
Measuring Employee Performance

Once you've hired the individual you believe will be the best asset to your company culture, you can breathe a sigh of relief. For the moment, your biggest problem has been solved. It's huge to have the burden of interviewing and choosing the perfect person for your position lifted from your shoulders. And, ideally, it should be a welcome relief for the employee, too, who has found a home with your company and no longer has to hunt down jobs that match his or her skills and needs.

Now you can go about *your* business in the company, and let your employee take care of the various responsibilities of his or her job description.

Fast forward a few months. Everything seems to be working out great. Your new executive administrative assistant is a great employee who is always looking to help others, pitching in to lighten the load when and where he or she can. One of his or her main roles is to meet and greet clients in a courteous professional manner. It's written precisely that way in the job description. Over time, though, you witness that your new administrative assistant appears to be disinterested, curt, or frustrated with clients. What would you do in this scenario?

1. Approach the employee at his or her desk and reprimand him or her then and there for talking inappropriately to clients.

2. Call the person into your office, thrust the job description in front of his or her face, and ask what part of "courteous and professional" does he or she not understand.

3. Document the performance issue and plan a face-to-face meeting one to two days later.

4. Walk away, pretending not to have heard the conversation.

5. Make a note each time the situation happens and put it in the employee's folder to discuss at his or her annual evaluation.

6. None of the above.

Answer honestly, and then come back after you've read the chapter and see if your answer remains the same.

Why Tracking and Evaluating Performance Are So Important

Remember that a big part of your business *is* your employees. Maintaining regular communication is important to make sure they are doing the job you expect them to be doing. Checking in with new employees—or old ones, for that matter—from time to time and discussing any of the responsibilities listed on their job description is the best way to make absolutely sure you're all on the same page. Employer–employee communication should happen informally, in conversations and group meetings, and formally, through regular performance evaluations.

Some people shudder at the mere mention of performance evaluations, no matter whether they are the evaluator or the one being evaluated. It's unfathomable to me why this valuable tool is met with so much resistance and dread. If you don't understand why you need to do performance evaluations, you can't expect your employees to embrace them.

Measuring employee performance is crucial to the success of a company and its employees. The bottom line is this: Laying out expectations clearly lays the foundation for a successful relationship. Your job description and your offer letter have laid out those expectations. However, both employer and employee need to evaluate whether those expectations are in fact being met.

Even with a thorough job description, there's room for miscommunication. Employees may sometimes find themselves in roles in which they're doing things they didn't expect, or an employer expects things that weren't clear to the employee. Communication and proactive evaluations can clear up these misunderstandings before they become actual issues.

Tips for Addressing or Handling Performance Issues

1. Be sure your employees are aware that performance evaluations are part of the job. Your offer letter should contain some language indicating this.

2. Be positive when you verbally communicate about the need for and value of your employee performance evaluations. In some larger companies, managers groan about having to do performance evaluations, making them seem trivial at best and a negative waste of time at worst. If evaluations are approached and performed correctly, this couldn't be further from the truth.

3. Recognition of an employee's performance should be *ongoing,* not solely through formal evaluations.

4. Maintain frequent communication to be able to properly evaluate employees. You can't ignore someone for six months and then expect to do a reasonable evaluation by spending a few minutes with him or her.

5. Often, employers in larger companies and corporations fail to do adequate performance evaluations because assessments are performed

annually, which is entirely too long a period of work to properly review as a whole. The evaluation tends to really only be about the last three to four months of the employee's performance. If you choose to do yearly evaluations, you must keep adequate notes throughout the year to be able to address an employee's performance fully. I do staff evaluations every six months because three months fly by in the small business world, and once a year is not enough! Use the structure that works for you. You should correct mistakes immediately and praise immediately.

6. Keep your performance evaluation simple. Use the offer letter and job description rather than a complicated template. This makes it easy and transparent for both sides to assess whether expectations are being met, and, hopefully, exceeded.

7. A formal performance evaluation is an opportunity to talk about the big picture and goals for the coming months or year. Major issues should be discussed throughout the year.

8. There should never be any surprises during a performance evaluation. It *should not* be the time when an employee first learns about specific concerns related to his or her work. You should address issues when they happen. So, if your employee did not have the end-of-month report on your desk by the deadline, assuming deadlines and responsibilities were clear in the job description, the time to address this issue is not three months later at a formal evaluation. It is when the infraction occurs.

9. A proactive, inclusive method of using performance evaluations allows employees to feel like part of the process. Many managers ask employees to fill out their own evaluations first and then go over them together. This gives employees a chance to reflect on their own work, eliminating some of the natural instinct to get defensive or angry. Personally, I don't like a lot of personal evaluation. Employees really care about what you think, not what they think of themselves. I am more apt to have them be really involved in setting their own professional goals during the evaluation. Then management can discuss these goals and align them with the company goals.

10. A performance evaluation should never leave an employee feeling demoralized. Many supervisors and high-level managers advise that the evaluation form be used as a guide to converse with an employee about performance. Some managers will never give the highest score in any category. If that's the case, cross out that number so employees understand that nothing about their own performance has kept them from achieving it. You can take away initiative by being cavalier with numbers.

Ignoring the Problem Won't Make It Go Away

It really is best to address problems related to performance immediately, even though confrontation is uncomfortable for most small business employers who do not have any solid HR background to draw from. Allowing an issue to go on too long before addressing it will only make it more of an issue. Although your reflex might be to ignore or run from conflict and confrontation, if you see an employee do something, or not do something, that has a negative impact on your work culture, other employees probably see it too. It may have even happened many times that you didn't see. If you see an issue and don't address it, you risk losing respect as a leader of your team.

As an employer, you are responsible for talking with employees about areas in which you feel they are not meeting expectations. This can only help employees do their job better.

Don't sweep problems under the rug or be afraid to call an employee out when there is a problematic situation. Just know how to do it properly and effectively.

Addressing a performance issue doesn't have to be complicated. Following these few simple steps will help you find your footing.

- Document the details: What did you see and hear, or what is being reported? When did it happen?

- Be proactive instead of reactive. Don't have a knee-jerk reaction to situations. Take some time to think about what you are going to say. I call this my

Parking Lot. I park the problem and think about it—for a minute, an hour, maybe a day—and then develop a plan for how to address it.

- Although cooler heads prevail, don't take too long, or the message could lose its value.

Let's revisit that earlier scenario in which the employee is not performing up to expectations. As part of her job description, she is to meet and greet walk-in clients, answer phone calls, and follow the company standards and practices that you have laid out. In my own company, the nature of our business draws numerous phone calls from people who ask questions over and over, and often repeat questions, which can be frustrating. And although we have a policy that requires applicants to apply online, we receive walk-in candidates from time to time. My own handling of this situation with an employee who was not doing the job that she was expected to do was to first realize that some performance issues needed to be addressed. Rather than stand over her desk and reprimand her for mishandling things, I took the time to write down my concerns, as well as what I expected of her. This happened on a Thursday. I processed the situation in my mind over the weekend and determined that her lack of experience and her young age were contributing to her manner in handling contentious and frustrating situations, and that it was my responsibility to help her.

I called her into my office for a meeting on the following Tuesday. This is pretty much how the meeting went:

Me: "We think the world of you here at Part-Time Pros. We want to see you grow in our company; however, to do that you have to prove yourself in the role that you're in, and currently you're not meeting my expectations.

"Here's what I'm seeing. (I stated my facts and gave her examples of conversations I'd heard her have with clients.)

"Here's what I expect. (I gave her examples of how she should address those situations.)

"Now, tell me your side. What did you see and feel when these situations presented themselves?"

What she revealed was that she was trying to lighten the workload for other staff members by taking on more responsibility with clients. She delivered bad news to disqualified applicants, although she didn't have the skills for that type of confrontation, which was actually part of the recruiter's job description. As for walk-in clients, she was adhering to company standards and practices.

In the end, we had an incredibly positive talk that showed me her value as an employee. I clarified her role and what was expected of her. Together we developed solutions to improve her performance and give her the skills to stay poised under pressure, creating scenarios that challenged her and how she should address them. Had I not taken the time to hear her side, we both would have missed on an opportunity to learn and grow. Never underestimate the power of listening.

The following excerpt from that performance evaluation will show you how valuable this process is. I simply documented this in a word document and had her sign.

EMPLOYEE PERFORMANCE EVALUATION

10/10/11- First Disciplinary Action Meeting

It has come to our attention that the way in which applicants are greeted and directed is not meeting our expectations. Brett and I met with (Employee) on October 10th to talk about her performance and discussed ways in which she could improve her customer service.

Here is what we have observed and what has been brought to our attention by clients and applicants. These topics served as the foundation for our conversation:

There have been complaints about the manner in which a person drops in and wishes to apply with Part-Time Pros. One client in particular, who walked in to apply, was told that we take applications online only and that walk-in interviews are not allowed.

A better approach would be to say, "Thank you for coming in. We do interviews by appointment only; however, since you are here, I will gladly scan a copy of your résumé, and if you would like to use one of our computers, you can complete the online application, and I can attach your résumé to your file. I can also look on our senior recruiter's calendar to see when she has a space open for an interview, and we can go ahead and schedule you. I can also see if our recruiting specialist is free to ask you a few questions." We want to always *seek to understand* their position and to try to go the extra mile to be kind, courteous, and respectful.

(Employee) said that since there are now kiosks to allow someone to apply, this approach was much better and would be received as more helpful by the applicants.

(Employee) has been "irritated" by candidates who "don't listen" to her instructions.

The candidate is our product and our client. Without good professionals, we are unable to complete jobs. The office manager must always be the one to help applicants, no matter how many times they call.

There have been a few instances when someone who is late for an appointment is told, "We have a policy that if you are late you can be deactivated from our system." It is unnecessary to share this information with an applicant. This type of information can be relayed in your first impression score, and the recruiters will consider it if they were to place the applicant.

(Employee) recognized that her frustration can be viewed by all. We will work together to develop tools and techniques to more professionally and appropriately work through these frustrations.

(Employee) also shared that she often felt it was her responsibility to communicate our standards to our candidates. We assured her that this was not the case and that all confrontational conversations should be conducted between the applicant and the senior recruiter or management. (Employee's) role as office manager is to be the applicant advocate and helpful in every way possible. I followed up with the recruiting staff to avoid them asking (Employee) to conduct any of the conversations with applicants.

(Employee's) lack of conversation while someone is waiting for an interview.

(Employee) is the client's first impression of Part-Time Pros. Just as she gives the applicant a first impression score, they give her and us a first impression score. The energy level needs to be high, positive, and cheerful. Life can be stressful and exhausting, but it is up to us to make a fabulous first impression. Every applicant should be greeted with a smile, a friendly greeting, and an offer to get some water or be of service, not "I need a copy of your license." Activity should be paused to greet someone.

(Employee) recognized this and will make a more conscious effort to be more friendly and outgoing to applicants.

(Employee's) tone of voice and shortness on the phone.

There have been instances in which we have witnessed (Employee) answering the phone and sounding as though she would rather be anywhere but there. She appears to be irritated by having to answer the phone. All calls should be answered with a cheerful, upbeat, and happy tone.

(Employee) and I talked about now answering the phone in the following manner: "Thank you for calling Part-Time and Tulsa-Med Pros, how may I help you?" instead of "Part-Time Pros and Tulsa-Med Pros."

(Employee) showing frustration while gathering payroll hours.

(Employee) wants to be able to do things for Brett, but we discussed the need for her to communicate when there are issues and let Brett handle them when needed.

(Employee) and Brett will talk more frequently if there is a payroll issue.

Billable hours are the only way Part-Time Pros makes money and can grow. People must be paid and be paid correctly. We recognize that it can be frustrating at times to repeatedly babysit candidates to submit time sheets; however, we need the hours to invoice so that we can pay our expenses. In the future, (Employee) should not share her frustration outwardly with staff. (Employee) should communicate all walls or roadblocks to Brett in private.

In our offer letter for this position, point #3 states "greeting and directing all visitors, clients, and job candidates with dignity and respect." We expect this to be done and are willing to invest time to ensure that (Employee) has the right customer service skills and training to be successful. We believe in (Employee) and believe that she can grow with Part-Time Pros. However, to be considered for any future openings, she needs to prove that 1) she is capable of providing exceptional customer service to our applicants and clients, 2) that she can control her emotions and 3) that candidates and clients are unaware of any potential frustrations she might have.

Without candidates, we do not have a company. We must welcome everyone who comes into the office or calls on the phone happily and cheerily, and be willing to help. We want (Employee) to remember that even though she has said the same thing a thousand times, it is the first time a given candidate may have heard it. Welcoming the candidate takes precedence over payroll, job postings, e-mails, everything.

The office manager is the face and voice of Part-Time Pros. (Employee) must remember that and be as positive and friendly as possible every time with every interaction.

Things we need to implement:

1. Allowing walk-ins to fill out an online application on one of the testing computers.

2. Offering coffee and/or water to waiting candidates.

3. Allowing candidates to talk on their phones while waiting.

Solutions:

1. Over the next 30 days, Carey Baker will work with (Employee) to help her gain the skills and techniques to handle various situations.

    a. (Employee) needs to submit some situations that have arisen that have been stressful or contentious to Carey by October 28th.

    b. Carey and (Employee) will review the list and determine some best practice responses.

2. (Employee's) performance will be re-evaluated on November 30th or sooner.

3. If performance has not improved, it may lead to further disciplinary action.

4. The goal of Part-Time Pros is to address and correct any poor performance as quickly as possible. We hope that (Employee) knows that if we did not feel confident that she could handle this feedback and make some changes, we would not be having this conversation. We would simply find a replacement.

5. We believe in (Employee) and her capabilities and want to see her perform at the level that we know she is capable of.

_____

(Employee)   Carey Baker

In order to have a thorough record of what transpired, I asked for a written response to the evaluation. Here are her comments:

In our meeting regarding my performance, I honestly felt comfortable. I know that you appreciate me and my work. Having the ability to come to you with concerns about the office or personal issues that impact me daily makes working here that much more enjoyable.

In the meeting we went over some issues where you felt that I was not meeting your expectations. While it may not be enjoyable being told you are doing something wrong or badly, I appreciated having my attitude addressed.

Sometimes I find myself jaded by the day to day dealings with candidates and their repetitive questions, and I can dwell on that. Having someone address it in a nice manner pushes me to do better. Also, knowing that you do support me and want me to do the best I can helped the overall morale of the meeting. Having the open dialogue and being able to explain my side of the story also made the meeting feel more motivational than disciplinary.

After the meeting, receiving the form about what was discussed was a good way to review and know what is expected from me moving forward. Also knowing that it would impact future growth let me know that in order for advancement, you wanted to see that I could take the direction and apply to my work.

Overall, I left the meeting knowing that changes needed to be made, and which changes you wanted me to make. It made me step back and realize that every time I am asked the same question, it is that person's first time to ask that question. I was reminded that I needed to put myself in the applicants' shoes and know that the question is not being asked to drive me nuts, but because they need to know how the system works.

I documented what I needed to talk with her about, and then added her feedback and concerns into the document. We both signed it and I placed a copy in her employee file.

While the written evaluation may appear very long and does go into great detail, once I had taken the necessary time to determine how I would address the issues, the remainder of the process, from discussion to resolution to documentation, took less than two hours. Using a template will only complicate the process. It's much simpler to write out the problem(s) one by one, in clear language, refer to the existing job description for the details of the expected performance, and address ways in which the behavior should be corrected.

Measuring performance is that easy. It really can be a positive, uplifting experience if it's handled right.

Don't Overlook Good Performance

Part of tracking an employee's performance is also acknowledging those things and those occasions when the employee performs very well. Not things that are expected, like showing up to work on time. But when the employee to whom you gave constructive criticism handles situations and tasks accordingly, recognize the individual for it right away. If employees perform certain aspects of their job beyond your expectations, take on an extra project, pick up the slack for a sick coworker, or make a valuable suggestion, absolutely praise their exceptional conduct. Praise them immediately, in the moment, when it will be greatly appreciated, and the impact will be so much greater.

If you're lucky enough to have an employee who just regularly goes above and beyond, note the level of dedication to work in the employee's file. You may not remember everything he or she did when it comes time for a formal evaluation. You don't want to miss the opportunity to recognize exceptional work ethics, or worse, run the risk of losing an exceptional employee because you failed to appreciate his or her best efforts.

I don't know anybody who doesn't enjoy receiving a compliment or being recognized for good work. If it makes you happy to see it, it stands to reason that your employee will be happy to hear about it. We're all human.

When All Else Fails

More often than not, being proactive by laying out expectations, tracking employee performance, communicating regularly, and addressing issues as they arise will result in a productive, performance-driven work culture.

Not everyone will act and react in ways you anticipate or desire, though. Your evaluation of an employee may fall on deaf ears. Or worse, the employee may be defensive about your assessment of his or her performance. For the most part, these situations can be managed. It's all about the delivery.

As an employer, you need to have empathy and be sensitive to what you're saying to your employee and to how well your comments are being received. I am not suggesting you sugarcoat any issues you need to address. It's so important that you are always honest and transparent. However, if you sense an employee is overly sensitive to your criticism, you can say something positive along with it: "I'm having this conversation with you because I value you as an employee and want to figure out how to improve this issue so we can grow together as a team."

Unfortunately, at some point you are probably going to have to deal with poor performance issues that aren't being resolved.

Here are the standard practices I follow to deal with an ineffective employee:

Step 1: Counseling Session/Review Meetings

This is a proactive way to encourage good performance and should involve a formal sit-down, one-on-one meeting with the employee and any supervisors.

- Discuss the employee's job and performance.

- During this conversation, put the employee at ease and stress the importance of the team.

- Pull up documentation such as a job description, company mission, vision, etc., to enforce why it is imperative that the employee address areas that need improvement.

- Keep the conversation on job performance and job requirements.

- Document each review and have all participants sign.

Step 2: Verbal/Written Notification

- When there is a problem, write out what it is and what you need to resolve the problem.

- Schedule a private meeting and use your written documentation as an outline for the conversation. Describe the performance issue and then ask the employee to explain his or her actions before deciding how to proceed.

- Don't underestimate the power of listening, but also stand your ground and clearly lay out expectations.

- Be firm but upbeat, and always try to express confidence in the employee's ability to turn things around.

- Document the meeting and have the employee sign and date all documentation. If the employee refuses to sign, state that he or she refused to sign and ask a witness (typically a supervisor) to sign.

Step 3: Probation or Suspension

I have never practiced this step because I do not have the time or the money to afford it but this step may be appropriate for others. Use your best judgement. This is necessary if Step 2 does not effectively correct the problem.

- Management must always be notified of this step.

- Conduct a face-to-face meeting and include members of management.

- Describe the current state of the employee's performance and again allow the employee to explain.

- Tell the employee that he or she is going to be suspended or that you are giving a "final" warning in lieu of suspension. I am more of an advocate for a final warning than suspension.

- Keep the turnaround time short—two weeks to one month, maximum. Small business owners cannot afford to keep an employee who is failing to perform. The entire team looks to management to see what behavior is acceptable and what is not acceptable. It is up to management to lead.

- Document the meeting and have all parties sign.

Step 4: Discharge

This is what all managers hope to avoid. I detest terminating employees. Personally, I view it as a failure on my part, but when all else fails, you need to know how to take this difficult yet necessary step.

- Conduct the meeting in private, but you should typically always have at least two members of management in attendance. Try to avoid doing it alone.

- Take into consideration whether special physical or security measures are appropriate and prepare accordingly, that is, remote log-in access, keys, alarm codes, whether the person has an aggressive attitude.

- Make sure your words and actions protect the employee's dignity and privacy.

- Tell the employee about the discharge decision and explain any exit procedures, payroll/benefits, how you will handle his or her personal property, etc.

- Keep the conversation as brief as possible since all of your reasons behind the termination decision have already been well documented in Steps 2 and 3.

- Obtain any company property and escort the employee out.

- Many companies think Friday is the best day to terminate; however, numerous studies show that Mondays or Tuesdays are best because this allows the discharged employee an opportunity to begin 'hitting the pavement' to other agencies or businesses instead of having a weekend to stew and worry.

- And lastly, DOCUMENT everything.

A Final Word about Performance Evaluations

A good boss does his or her best to ensure that the performance evaluation process doesn't leave an employee feeling demoralized. Many supervisors and high-level managers advise that the evaluation form be used as a guide to conversing with an employee about performance. Some managers never give the highest score in any category. If that's the case, cross out that number so employees understand that nothing about their own performance has kept them from achieving it. You can take away initiative by being cavalier with numbers.

A proactive, inclusive method of using performance evaluations allows employees to feel like part of the process. Many managers ask employees to fill out their own evaluations first and then go over them together. This gives employees a chance to reflect on their own work, eliminating some of the natural instinct to get defensive or angry.

Your performance evaluation plan should always tie into your company's core values and mission. When you have those intact, you can more easily assess how your employees are doing in meeting those standards. Here is a sample of my company's mission and vision plan:

The Mission and Vision of Part-Time Pros

Our Mission

"to provide the perfect match between client needs, desires, and wants with associate knowledge, skills, and abilities."

Our Vision

"We do more than just fill jobs; we create them"

Our Core Values

Balance – Provide healthy, flexible work/life balance.

Efficiency – Pursue the most efficient and effective methods to engage our clients, our associates, and ourselves through the use of technology.

Accountability – Strive always to do the right thing, with our clients and associates' best interest at heart, pursuing the highest ethical standards to reach our goals.

Professional – Present the organization and ourselves in the most sincere and transparent way possible.

Respect – Working together and valuing our individual differences makes us a more creative and cohesive team.

Ownership – Vested in the success of the organization so that our actions and behaviors reflect the intrinsic value we receive when placing talented associates. In return, our stake grows in the shared success we will enjoy.

With these key values in place, managers are better equipped to evaluate their team knowing the overall expectations that staff should be striving to meet while doing their job, as well as establishing a plan for developing an employee's growth within the company. Following is the actual Employee Development process and forms I use in my company. This one ties into the job description for an executive administrative assistant we used earlier, but it can be used for every position within your company. I would like to credit Kent Williams with HRB for his help. He worked with me to create a perfect performance and development plan that fit my needs today.

Performance and Development Steps

Section 1. Review Job Description on Page 1. Please add any new duties and responsibilities you are currently performing and cross out any duties that are no longer relevant to your role. Please bring your edits to the Performance and Development meeting set for **(insert date)**.

Section 2. Goal Setting. During our review on (insert date), we will discuss personal and professional goals as well as share with you Part-Time Pros and Tulsa-Med Pros' goals for 2012. Please come prepared to begin a discussion about your 2012 goals. Please submit your goals one week before the review.

Section 3. Self-Assessment. Please complete the self-assessment questions listed in this Performance and Development plan and provide answers to Carey Baker one week before the review. We will discuss these answers during our meeting on **(insert date)**.

Section 4. Evaluation on Core Values and Core

Competencies. This section will be completed by Brett and Carey Baker and will be reviewed during our meeting on (insert date). A copy is being provided to you so that you know what to expect.

SECTION 1 JOB DESCRIPTION REVIEW

EXECUTIVE ADMINISTRATIVE ASSISTANT

Job Description

Reports to: President

Salary: $20.00/hour

Position Type: Full-Time Non-exempt

JOB SUMMARY

Local company is seeking a full-time executive administrative assistant to work in corporate office. The professional hired will provide administrative assistance to the President of the company. The person hired will work with minimal instruction or supervision.

ESSENTIAL FUNCTIONS

Drafts correspondence, memoranda, etc., for internal and/or external distribution.

Coordinates all travel for the President.

May prepare agendas and materials related thereto, and see that all legal requirements are met.

Conserves the President's time by reading, researching, and routing correspondence.

Responsible for establishing and maintaining official documents and records in appropriate files.

May be asked to attend some meetings, seminars, etc., possibly to take notes or furnish information.

May do research for a project.

Maintains office supplies inventory by checking stock to determine inventory level, anticipating needed supplies, evaluating new office products, placing and expediting orders for supplies, verifying receipt of supplies.

May receive visits or calls regarding complaints that may be resolved or referred to proper person for resolution.

Provides coverage for other assistants when/if needed.

Cleans out e-mail and corresponds on behalf of the President.

Takes dictation.

Runs personal errands for the President when needed.

Keeps accurate and organized calendars and assists the President in preparing for meetings.

Performs any necessary follow-up for the President after meetings.

Performs such other duties as may be assigned.

KNOWLEDGE, SKILLS, AND ABILITIES

Thorough knowledge of modern office practices and procedures and the use of computers, office machines, and equipment.

Ability to understand and interpret pertinent policies and procedures clearly and accurately.

Ability to establish and maintain effective working relationships with supervising personnel, coworkers, subordinates, the media, representatives from all levels of government, civic organizations, business professionals, and the public.

Ability to project a positive, concerned image to the public.

Ability to communicate effectively orally and in writing.

Sufficient skill in typing and the ability to take sufficient notes at a meeting to prepare an accurate record of events.

Excellent organizational skills.

Better-than-average attendance.

TRAINING AND EXPERIENCE

Advanced training in typing and general office procedures.

5+ years experience performing administrative duties.

Bachelor's degree.

Proficient in Microsoft Office Suite—Outlook, PowerPoint, Excel, Publisher, and Word.

COMPANY CONFORMANCE STATEMENT

When performing the respective tasks and duties, the employee hired will be expected to conform to the following:

Perform quality work within deadlines with or without supervision.

Interact professionally with other employees, customers, and suppliers.

Work effectively as a team contributor on all assignments.

Work independently while understanding the need for communicating and coordinating work efforts with other employees and organizations.

PHYSICAL REQUIREMENTS

Physical requirements for positions include arm and hand steadiness and finger dexterity enough to use a keyboard and telephone; occasional lifting up to 25 pounds; may be subject to walking, standing, sitting, and reaching; and vision, speech, and hearing sufficient to perform the essential tasks. Any physical restrictions should be discussed or noted within the interview process.

COMMENTS

SECTION 2 GOAL SETTING

Part-Time Pros' Goals for 2012:

List of goals the company has created: This is a chance for management to communicate the company's direction as well as tie everyone's job back to the company goals.

Discussion on Goals for Employee to Accomplish in 2012:

Project Goal:

Target Completion Date:

Project Goal:

Target Completion Date:

Project Goal:

Target Completion Date:

SECTION 3 SELF–ASSESSMENTS

List your most significant accomplishments or contributions in the past year.

a.

b.

c.

d.

List the events/meetings you have attended to represent Part-Time Pros/Tulsa-Med Pros in the community. These events are not required work-related events:

a.

b.

c.

d.

Looking to the future, where do you see yourself in the Part-Time Pros/Tulsa-Med Pros organization in the next three years?

What can we do to enhance your career development and help us achieve Part-Time Pros/Tulsa-Med Pros' goals?

Describe any challenges that make it difficult for you to effectively fulfill your responsibilities.

Professional and Personal Development Question

What areas would you like to improve and develop? What are your plans to accomplish this?

What I want to improve and develop	How I am going to achieve this

SECTION 4 CORE VALUES EVALUATION — BE A PRO

This performance evaluation form is designed to link employee performance to Part-Time Pros and Tulsa-Med Pros' mission and core values. The form should be used to summarize and assess the employee's overall performance for the past year, to establish results to be achieved for specific task or projects for the next year, and to identify development goals to enable the employee to enhance performance in his or her current position or to prepare him or her for future growth. The written assessment should not replace ongoing feedback and communication regarding job performance.

Performance Levels

Performance Rating Scale	Definition	Rating
Exceeds Expectations	Consistently exceeds performance standards. Provides leadership, fosters teamwork, is highly productive, innovative, and responsive, and generates top-quality work.	3
Meets Expectations	Meets performance standards. Seldom exceeds or falls short of desired results.	2
Does Not Meet Expectations	Falls short of performance standards.	1

BALANCE	1	2	3	TOTAL
Maintains a healthy work/life balance				
Looks for opportunities to help others so that they may have a balance				
Manages priorities for work and family that support balance, achieve results, and reduce stress				

EFFICIENCY	1	2	3	TOTAL
Pursues the most efficient and effective methods to engage our clients, associates, and self through use of technology				
Maximizes each day to ensure that progress is made to grow professionally and personally				
Eliminates day-to-day distractions to maximize time in office and productivity				

ACCOUNTABILITY	1	2	3	TOTAL
Strives always to do the right thing, with our clients and associates' best interests at heart, pursuing the highest ethical standards to reach our goals				
Able to admit mistakes and work toward a better solution				
Delivers on promises, sticks to deadlines, and supports coworkers with team spirit				

PROFESSIONAL	1	2	3	TOTAL
Pro at presenting the organization and us in the most sincere and transparent way possible				
Maintains high ethical standards and professional standards				
Presents professional image and exhibits professional communication				

RESPECT	1	2	3	TOTAL
Works to honor and respect different perspectives, experiences, cultures, and traditions				
Demonstrates respect for others through active listening and open communication				
Treats others with courtesy, politeness, and kindness				

OWNERSHIP	1	2	3	TOTAL
Vested in the success of the organization so that our actions and behaviors reflect the intrinsic value we receive when placing talented associates				
Takes on a leader/owner mentality when approaching customers and applicants				
Looks for ways to improve processes, enhance relationships, and grow the business				

CORE COMPETENCIES: In addition to our core values, Part-Time Pros has identified a few core competencies that all employees must adhere to for the company to grow and be successful.

PRODUCTIVITY AND DEPENDABILITY	1	2	3	TOTAL
Conscientious, responsible, and reliable in adhering to work schedules and deadlines, as well as attendance. Willingly accepts additional assignments when called upon				
COMMUNICATION	**1**	**2**	**3**	
Exchanges information in a timely manner, listens and understands, uses confidential information with discretion; effectively writes and/ or speaks clearly and concisely with persons at all levels				

CUSTOMER SERVICE	1	2	3	TOTAL
Listens carefully and responds to customer requests and problems; delivers friendly, courteous service to internal and external customers; demonstrates a commitment to increasing customer satisfaction				
PROBLEM SOLVING AND JUDGEMENT	1	2	3	
Understands how various issues and problems interrelate, anticipates problems, demonstrates ability to examine issues in new ways, uses logic and good judgment to reach solutions				
INTEGRITY	1	2	3	
Maintains high ethical principles and professional standards while exhibiting integrity and honesty in all aspects of work				
COMPASSION	1	2	3	
Shows compassion toward applicants and exhibits empathy to those seeking work; also listens to others' point of view by expressing understanding of their needs and concerns				

Employee Comments:

SECTION 3

Keeping a Good Employee

I've said this repeatedly in conversations with my own employees, clients, and applicants: When I hire people, my goal is for them to remain with my company for the next 30 years. That's not an exaggeration on my part, nor is it an unrealistic expectation. Although some positions have a natural turnover, for the most part I hire with the intention of keeping employees satisfied in their jobs or desiring to grow within our company. If you don't spend sufficient time thinking about how to accomplish that, you will revisit the hiring process more times than you probably want to.

It isn't enough to merely provide an individual with a job. Yes, in tougher economic times it may be easier for employers to adopt the philosophy that they're doing employees a favor, and it's not uncommon for employees to feel grateful to even have a job. I urge you, as a small business owner, to be more professional and humane than that. You certainly don't view your employees doing their jobs as them doing you a favor, so don't fool yourself into thinking that you are doing one for them. As for gratitude, employees shouldn't be grateful for fair exchange of their services for a paycheck. They will, however, be very grateful for a work environment that is productive, pleasant, consistent, realistic, fair, and respectful. This is the type of atmosphere that will help you keep a good employee.

You know how valuable your employees are to your business. They are the face of your company. When you are on the hiring side of the work process, and you find an individual who meets your needs and then performs well in your organization, you want to be every bit as appealing to him or her as the individual was to you when you first interviewed. I don't mean you have to throw a party or hand out big bonuses. The everyday things make all the difference.

1. Provide a good work/life balance

When your employees have other interests and things to do outside of punching the clock at your business, they will be more fulfilled. The more fulfilled your employees are personally, the better they will perform professionally. Employees who perform well in their jobs are more likely to remain satisfied with the company they work for.

When you initially hire your employees, you do so based on the impression they made during your interview process, when you likely found out a little about their personal lives and interests. Long before your employees began working for you, they had people and things that were important to the foundation of their life. That doesn't end just because they now work for you. Your business, while it should be important to them, is not the be all and end all of their existence.

As an employer, you should encourage a balance between an employee's work life and personal life. Sure, it's wonderful to have a dedicated employee who is committed to his or her personal success and to the success of your company. However, if an employee is sacrificing too much on a personal level, it's really not going to turn out well for your business. At some point, you are bound to end up with a burnt-out and resentful employee. For example, if you hire someone who is a self-professed fitness buff and has a family, and he or she is arriving to work very early and often staying late, odds are that something else is suffering because of that schedule. It's part of your job to make sure your employees maintain balance. You may have to step in and send them home early, or hire support, or evaluate their workload.

Employees tend to have greater loyalty toward employers who show an interest in the big picture of their lives, and not merely in the bottom line of the business. My senior recruiting manager works far more hours than I would like her to work, and I worry that sometimes she's not keeping that work/life balance. Although she is a very big reason our company has grown, I try to implement balance in her life as much as possible, allowing her to work from home when she needs to and supporting her interests in outside activities and organizations. I know that taking care of my own personal needs makes me a better boss, a better wife, and a better mom, so why wouldn't I want the same for my staff?

Give your employees permission to "turn it off." Take a walk around the office at 5 p.m.—or whatever time your workday ends. Tell your employees it's quitting time and to go home to their families and their lives. My husband does this regularly, and it's one of the things my staff truly appreciates. The fact is, there comes a time in the workday when, physically and mentally, an employee is not going be at his or her best. After working a certain number of hours, your staff is just not as productive anymore. It's better for them and for your business if they take time to recharge, so that they want to and are able to give you their best effort.

2. Lead by example

Begin with a good start to the workday

How do you come into work every morning? Do you rush in, already trying to wrap your head around the many pressing concerns of the day? Are you talking on your cell phone? Do you walk directly into your office and close the door so you can drink your coffee while you plan your day? Whether you realize this or not, actions like these unintentionally give off negative energy. I am usually the last person to arrive at the office each morning. When I come in, I make it a point to say "good morning" to everyone before I go to my desk. It's simple common courtesy, really. You wouldn't walk into your home and not greet your family or arrive at a party and not acknowledge the other guests immediately. Taking a few minutes to acknowledge and communicate with your staff sets the right tone for the day. While you may think the opposite, staff members who interact are more likely to feed off one another and be more productive. Your leading by example will help encourage that communication.

Make a conscious effort to be positive

Your demeanor affects your whole team. Actually, the demeanor of everyone in your office affects the entire staff, but since you are "the boss," your attitude is the most significant. To quote a line from the movie *Remember the Titans,* "Attitude reflects leadership." Your attitude becomes your employees' attitude. You can't expect your staff to be upbeat and hardworking and doing the right thing if you're not.

Think not only about *what* you say but also *how* you say it. Strive to make the words that come out of your mouth positive ones. Instead of a mumbled "Hey" as you pass an employee's desk on your way in, try a smile and "Happy Monday!" Rather than a sigh and a monotone "I'm okay," try an upbeat response when someone asks how you are. Attitude is contagious, and you want to spread around as much positive energy as you can so your staff will catch it, too. Even seemingly trivial comments like, "It's hot as hell outside," for example, create a sense of negativity. However, if you say, "Let's all go outside and see if you can really fry an egg on a hot sidewalk," you make the same point with a much lighter tone, creating a much lighter mood.

Show that you aren't afraid to get your hands dirty

Rolling up your sleeves and showing that you aren't above doing what needs to be done is a great example for your employees. When you show them that no job is beneath you and take interest in issues that arise, your employees will appreciate the respect you show for their individual jobs.

My company, like many staffing agencies, has established standards and qualifications that candidates must meet before we will refer them for jobs. One particular gentleman was upset with our response to his application and challenged our standards. He sent us a negative, nasty e-mail because we had disqualified him from consideration for employment based on our standards. Understandably, my staff just wanted to ignore him and move on from this situation, especially since the man's comments more or less proved our assessment accurate. However, one of the most important parts of my job as a business owner and an employer is to *seek to understand*.

I wanted this applicant to know that his assumptions about our business were incorrect. I wanted to show him that we care and take great pride in what we do, which is why we have those standards and practices in place. Though my time is extremely limited and my schedule packed, I took the time to send him a very positive e-mail response. I did this so my staff would see that they shouldn't shy away from confrontation, especially when we know we are doing the right thing. I also wanted my employees to know that I am as invested in the company as they are and willing to do the work, seek to understand candidates, and address any issues.

The time I spent on this negative situation was more than well spent, accomplishing three very positive results: 1) my staff saw I was willing to do any job that needed to be done, 2) the gentleman apologized directly to the staff member he had insulted, and 3) it set the stage for what I expect from my staff.

Recognize great performance

Recognizing employees is an essential building block for retaining employees. There is nothing complicated about recognition, but it continues to be one of the highest needs on employees' lists. Whether recognition is done verbally or through awards, the point is to extend praise regularly. Everyone needs a pat on the back every once in a while. You don't need to spend a lot of money, but an occasional pedicure, car detail, or lunch can go a long way in keeping your best employees with your company.

Understand who your employees are

With up to four different generations working together in the workforce today, employee relations aren't one size fits all. You could easily have two employees working the same job, but if one is a Baby Boomer and the other a Millennial, the way in which you manage them needs to be completely different. They will not accomplish tasks in the same manner, but if you appreciate and respect each generation's approach, good employees will want to keep working for you, no matter their age.

Many articles, and indeed, entire books, have been devoted to generational differences. The information that follows was gleaned from a particularly insightful article on the Society for Human Resource Management (SHRM) website, which I encourage you to visit and read in its entirety. There is so much you can learn from it.

"Each generation's values manifest in workplace behaviors—such as communicating, managing others, getting work done and trying to move ahead," notes author Adrienne Fox. "Understanding and discussing generational differences—and stereotypes—can help prevent misunderstandings, set expectations, engender empathy and improve engagement."

- **The Silent Generation, or Traditionalists**, are the elders in today's workforce. They are frugal, adhere to rules, remain loyal to employers, and have a deep sense of responsibility and sacrifice for the good of the organization. They like to communicate via face-to-face meetings or phone calls and like to be recognized for their tenure, loyalty and the hours they work.

- **Baby Boomers** are associated with social consciousness and independence. They are not very accepting of differences or change. Many are working longer than they planned, partly because their assets have been depleted, and because their identities are tied to their careers. They are skilled at building rapport and relationships, and prefer face-to-face encounters.

- **Generation Xers** are self-reliant and used to doing everything themselves. They don't require a lot of hand-holding, just want to do their job, and are more likely to communicate via e-mail rather than meet in person or make phone calls. They became more tech savvy to find work. "Cynicism is often associated with Generation X, whose focus is on gaining transferable skills so that they can be ready when the rug is pulled out from under them—as it has throughout their lives. All the major institutions fell apart around them—marriage, family, corporations, and the economy. Their attitude is, "You've never done anything for me. Why should I do something for you?"

- **Millennials** want regular communication, no matter how it's delivered. Robert Half International and Yahoo! HotJobs polled more than 1,000 Millennials and found that more than 60 percent wanted to hear from managers at least once a day. Managing Millennials involves constant feedback and coaching. This generation has grown up with supportive parent–child relationships and likes to be mentored. Delegate and give them continuous feedback, and they will be happy. They view work/life flexibility as a necessity for long-term productivity and engagement. They like to be kept in the loop on executive decisions and business strategies. Acknowledge their enthusiasm for the work, ask them to write their own self-assessment, and then you can discuss any discrepancies.[1]

Allow opportunities for development

Showing an interest in employees' training is such a key factor in keeping them working for you. Although some employers may fear that the more training they provide, the more likely the employee will take those acquired skills elsewhere, that doesn't have to be the case.

If you hire great employees, they probably want stability and longevity as much as you do. To accomplish that, you want them to remain satisfied and happy. Employees who are encouraged to expand their personal and

---

1. Adrienne Fox, "Mixing It Up," *HR Magazine* 56, no. 5 (2011), http://www.shrm.org/Publications/hrmagazine/EditorialContent/2011/0511/Pages/0511fox.aspx

professional development appreciate their jobs. With few exceptions, everyone needs a break from the typical routine. Seminars and ongoing certification programs for your employees feed their personal development appetite. Even if a higher-level position isn't available for them to move into, allowing employees time to learn other skills, mentor, or take continuing education classes can help them grow as individuals. Encourage engagement with various associations to help foster growth. It is a win-win because employees often come back with great ideas to share.

For example, by supporting my senior recruiter's passion for volunteering at a ministry for professionals seeking employment, my company ended up finding a perfect match for an existing client. That's not the reason that I supported her interest, but it's a nice fringe benefit. In the long run, whatever you can do to help an employee grow will benefit your business. This shouldn't be your sole intention in offering growth opportunities, but it is proof that the positive cycle of give-and-take really does work.

Consider promotions carefully

All business owners I've ever talked to think that when a position is open in their company, they are obligated to promote an employee from within the company, because they want to create a business culture where their employees have the opportunity to grow. Although this idea seems to make perfect sense, it could end up backfiring on you. I should know. It happened to me.

My former office manager was truly an MVP employee. She could handle multiple tasks, paid incredible attention to detail, and made a great impression on our clients. I promoted her to a newly created position for which I had an idea what I wanted but not a specific laid-out job description (first mistake). I put her into a role that did not have many guidelines from the outset. The position turned out to involve a lot of phone work and monotonous, tedious tasks. The story does not end well. I had to fire my former MVP employee—a big reason why I wanted to write this book.

I place the blame for this squarely on my own shoulders. First, I assumed that since she had been with me the longest, I should give her the position, which came with more money and more responsibility. Second,

I failed to identify precisely what I needed in that newly created role. Had I laid out and presented the details of the job, my employee would have had the opportunity to review whether this was a position she truly wanted. Third, I assumed that she was bored in her current position. I did not maximize my performance meetings with her effectively enough to find out if she was satisfied with the job she was doing and what she wanted to focus on.

The lesson is simple. If you want to consider promoting internally, first know what the position you are hiring for entails. Then you can approach your existing employee and invite him or her to apply for it. Have your employee go through the application process just like anyone else. This way you will be able to determine if he or she actually has the ability to do the job.

Internal employees may feel slighted if they aren't automatically promoted to a position. Your goal, however, is to create a performance-driven culture where everyone is pulling his or her own weight and is given compensation tied to performance, and where there is no sense of entitlement and expectation simply because an employee has been with the company for a long time. To accomplish this, be transparent and communicate the following to your employees:

- Encourage them to apply for the job, but tell them that you will be hiring the best person with the best skills and capabilities to do that job.

- Tell them that the last thing you want to do is put them in a position to fail by placing them in a role not suited for them or that they aren't ready for.

- Speak openly and honestly. "I am looking for the person who is going to be the best fit for this position. I know you have been with me a very long time, and I want you to continue to be with me. However, the skills I need are X, and ultimately I need to hire the person with the strongest skills."

- If an employee does not have the skills for a position, tell the individual that you will work with him/her to develop a plan to obtain those skills. A perfect place for this is within the goals section of the performance plan I created.

Embrace workplace flexibility

With technology making it easier and easier to work from remote locations, there's little excuse for most businesses not to offer flexible schedules to accommodate employees' needs. As long as you effectively communicate expectations and your employee is delivering, it shouldn't matter if he or she has spent eight hours or six hours performing the job.

Flexibility ranks high on an employee's wish list. I began my business because of my frustration with the old-school mentality of my employers, who wanted me tied to the office between 8 and 5 p.m. daily, regardless if I was done at 4 p.m. or if the majority of my work could be done from home. Aside from jobs that require an on-site presence, such as receptionists or jobs that involve security issues, there's no reason for most businesses not to be flexible. In fact, there is every reason for them to be flexible.

Employees view flexibility as a sign that their employer sincerely cares about them as a person, which is at the top of their list for job satisfaction. They tend to stay with these employers longer and have a much higher level of productivity.

I am not suggesting that your employees can show up in the office whenever they feel like it. It's up to you as the manager to set expectations and guidelines. However, little things like not counting a sick day when employees have to take off two or three hours for a doctor's appointment or to drive their child to a tournament can really foster loyalty and longevity.

My senior recruiting manager used to work in an office at her former job, from 7:30 a.m. to 5:30 p.m. She was always very busy and had plenty to do, but felt constricted and overwhelmed in that environment. Because my company places so much importance on a work and life balance, and embraces technology, she can now work from home when she needs to. She feels better knowing that she can be home with a sick child and still manage her work responsibilities. Or she can call me and tell me that she's going to work from home because there are fewer distractions and she has a lot to do. Flexibility is one of the things she appreciates most about her job.

Don't confuse flexibility with fewer hours or less productivity. Employees who work from home often end up working more hours. They have more satisfaction while doing their work because they aren't as stressed about getting things done within a certain time frame.

Just be sure that you have the ability to track performance. I highly recommend some type of performance-tracking software that suits the needs of your business. From there, you can track whether goals are being met and generate reports to address issues with employees who may be abusing the privilege, or just to alleviate your own concerns when you see an employee frequently leaving at 3 p.m. If the report indicates that your employees are doing their jobs to your expectations, the issue disappears.

Seven Additional Ways to Keep Great Talent

1. Maintain great communication and clearly defined expectations

The most satisfied employees know exactly what is expected of them and what the ultimate outcome of a particular project or job description is. They know exactly what the big picture is for their position. For example, my recruiters are responsible for filling open jobs with the most qualified candidates possible. They know I track their success and look at the fill ratio each month. They also know that I allow them to find their own route toward these outcomes. I allow them to use their own styles and strengths, but I also give them processes to follow so that I am able to track their performance.

2. Allow employees to make a difference

When employees feel a sense of mission and purpose, their job has meaning and significance. They want to know they are contributing to an important endeavor. The best workplaces give their employees a sense of purpose, help them feel they belong, and enable them to make a difference.

3. Money does not always create happiness

Employees say money is actually in the middle of their list of top ten reasons to stay at a company. Management, work environment, people, and growth opportunities rate much higher than money and benefits. Fair compensation is necessary to attract great employees, but it is not always why they stay. More often than not, when I ask people why they are taking my call to hear about a new opportunity, the work environment and management are the #1 and #2 reasons.

4. Give feedback as often as possible

Regular feedback helps employees stay focused on their productivity. Weekly staff meetings are a great way to achieve this. Objective feedback helps employees continue to understand their roles. You should emphasize their strengths and how best to use them. This will help employees gain self-understanding and knowledge about the talents they possess and how those talents are applied every day at work.

5. Nurture friendships at the office

Human beings are social by nature. Work is a place where long-term friendships are often developed. This evolution of quality relationships between people is very normal and is part of a healthy workplace. Loyalties among your personnel can foster company loyalty. Set up an environment in which friendships can be developed and are able to grow. Have group outings every quarter to allow for some fun outside work. Be okay with you as the manager not being included in the circle. The boss or owner should care about his or her employees but has little business being close friends with staff.

6. Invest in the right tools

Simple things like adequate lighting, ergonomic furniture, product information guides, and networked computers allow your people to do their jobs right. In addition, software that allows them to boost productivity and performance will increase their satisfaction. How many times have you been frustrated because you had a task to complete but did not have the tools to get it done quickly? When we invested in a customer relationship management (CRM) system, it made life easier for everyone. It created greater efficiency and productivity, which promoted better balance.

7. Include employees in the decision-making process

Great employers consult with employees regularly to make sure their ideas and instincts are recognized. Especially when making decisions that affect an employee's position, making him or her part of the process is most important. In doing this, you acknowledge the employee's intelligence and value. When employees' opinions count, the employees feel a sense of pride and ownership.

Work atmosphere, the camaraderie of fellow employees and their managers, and continuing personal development opportunities are the primary reasons employees remain at a company. When these innate needs are met, employees tend to be much more productive, profits increase, and there is a greater level of customer satisfaction.

SECTION 4
How to Be a Good Boss

Being a good person and being a good boss don't necessarily go hand in hand.

There are plenty of *good* people in the world who just don't possess the essential characteristics, qualities, and traits of a good boss. Having a pleasant personality, going out of your way to be helpful, and being kind, considerate, and generous are all really great attributes, but leading, supervising, and managing your employees takes more than that. Don't get me wrong, though. A boss who is friendly and caring certainly appeals to employees, but don't underestimate the value of professionalism and all it entails.

On the other hand, just because an individual isn't exactly affable doesn't mean he or she isn't a good boss. There's certainly an abundant supply of socially inadequate managers who may not relate well personally to employees but know how to convey expectations and are organized and effective in their work.

Now, most people just are who they are. However, if you truly want to be a good boss, there are ways to assess yourself and steps you can take to implement changes in your approach to people and situations.

Some of these things are similar to what we've discussed in the previous section on keeping a good employee. The difference here is that the focus is on *you* as a boss and what you need to consider about yourself in that role. Employees and managers need to do their part to create work environments that are productive and positive.

Traits of a Good Boss

With the help of some respected professionals, both employees and employers, I've come up with a combination of positive personality traits and effective leadership skills that results in what most people would consider the ideal boss. Although most of these can be inherent qualities, each one can be learned at any point in life.

Is professional

No one expects you to change the crux of who you are. Some people are moody by nature. Some are overly enthusiastic. Everyone has "off" days when he or she just doesn't feel up to par. However, as a manager, you have to conduct yourself in a professional manner even when you don't really want to.

You are human and are bound to have a bad day every now and then. A sick child, car trouble, or personal problems can upset the apple cart, but your problems don't have to disrupt your entire team. Keeping your demeanor calm and focused instead of reactive during trying situations will set a good tone for your office atmosphere and a good example for your employees.

Being professional doesn't mean you can't be personal with your staff. If you have forged a relationship and care to share private details instead of bottling them up, go ahead. Just be sure to be appropriate. Don't rant and rave about the situation and put everyone else on edge. For particularly stressful situations, take a walk, go to the gym if you can, or anywhere else where you can release some steam. Just don't do it in the office, unless you are prepared for your staff to do the same when they're having a bad day. Remember, lead by example. How you conduct yourself becomes how others will conduct themselves.

Is approachable

Being a "people" person is a great inherent trait of a good boss. Some people are just so easy to be around; conversation and communication just come naturally. For others, approachability isn't a trait, but it can be a learned skill.

When it comes to your employees, adopt an "open door" policy where your staff can come to you, not only with problems and concerns but also with ideas or exciting news. Acting this way as the leader will foster greater communication among your team. If you set an environment in which you are unapproachable, you risk creating a "you vs. them" attitude among your team members, or worse, completely discouraging team interaction, which is bad for your business.

One HR generalist I know stressed that an approachable boss benefits employee productivity. She always had to go around her former boss to get the information she needed. That's just wrong. No matter how thorough you may be, there will occasionally be situations in which a staff member needs clarification or additional details regarding an assignment. If he or she isn't comfortable coming to you for that, the project will take longer to complete or be inaccurate.

Is honest and ethical

As obvious as this seems, it isn't always going to be easy for you to be honest—with your staff and with your clients. If your employees hear you lying to a client to address his or her dissatisfaction, they'll lose respect for you. If you promise potential employees the world at their interview and can't deliver, you will lose credibility. Telling the good, the bad, and the ugly is hard, but you'll be better off in the long run.

For example, if you are mentoring, open-minded, and communicative, by all means convey that in an interview with a potential employee you'd really like to work for your company. However, if that isn't your management style, don't mislead applicants and allow them to base their decision to work with you on false impressions. During a conversation about a former boss, one senior manager said it was as though his boss had read every how-to book on managing people, used all the right words in interviews, but never implemented the methods in his approach.

A good boss doesn't dangle carrots. If an employee you value receives a job offer from another organization, don't promise him or her a promotion in six months if you can't deliver on that promise. A great boss would never hold employees back. Even if it inconveniences you, never lie to them. Be honest about what you can and cannot do, and wish them well.

In addition, be careful not to place blame squarely on an employee in sticky situations, especially if it's to take the heat off you. A good boss is responsible for the actions of his or her team, and throwing an employee under the bus will destroy not only his or her trust in you but also that of the entire team.

Manages not to over-manage

You may have previously done some or all of the work you now delegate to your staff. There will be moments when you need to reel yourself in and remind yourself why you hired your employees. You needed help in those positions. The employees proved to you they were qualified to handle the job. Now, let them.

We've talked repeatedly about the need to clearly communicate and convey your expectations. Assuming you've done that, allow your employees the freedom to accomplish the tasks associated with their position in the best way they see fit. A "my way or the highway" attitude could end up with you doing all the work. Each member of your team has particular talents and skills, and preferred methods and processes for accomplishing tasks. As long as your employees are maintaining the company's standards and procedures, don't interfere.

One of my trusted clients recalls a boss whose relationship with her staff was more like a teacher–student relationship, which he viewed as condescending and not very professional.

As a good boss, you should demonstrate faith and confidence in the people you supervise.

If an employee's method really isn't working efficiently, offer insight into the process you know to be effective and give the employee the tools he or she needs. Then, get out of the way and let your employee do his or her job. Most of my employee and employer sources say that the best boss they've ever had let them do their work without micromanaging. As long as the employees completed their assignments and tasks in a timely manner, they appreciated being able to create their own schedule and work at their own pace.

Gives credit where it's due

Recognition has been highly ranked by employees as a factor in job satisfaction. I have mentioned the value of recognition previously, but I bring it up here for another reason. Sometimes managers and bosses are more in the limelight than their employees. When something positive is attributed to the company, bosses often receive—and take—all of the credit.

Don't steal your employees' thunder. If a member of your team has done something of merit that benefits the company, don't take credit for it. In addition to showing a lack of integrity, not giving your employees credit will lead your staff to stop striving to exceed goals and expectations since they know they won't be recognized for their hard work.

The best boss never lets his or her own ego get in the way and wants to push his or her employees out in front and let them have the applause. Employees respect and trust managers who act this way, and they want to continue to perform well for them.

Encourages development

A good boss wants his or her employees to be the absolute best they can be. This means acknowledging that there is more to employees than the job they are currently responsible for. Look at the bigger picture when considering your staff. If you have excellent employees who show real talent for the industry, encourage them to expand their professional growth. Offer training or mentoring; help employees recognize their own strengths and develop additional skills.

Appreciation of this trait is almost unanimous among the employees I've spoken with. One even credits her employer with helping her overcome her fear of returning to school and finally pursuing the additional training she had long desired.

Helping your employees recognize their own potential and fulfill their goals creates a positive atmosphere, one that makes your staff feel all the more engaged in the company.

Is engaged

This is an area in which employers generally assess their staff. However, the quality and level of your engagement with your employees don't go unnoticed.

During a scheduled one-on-one meeting with an employee, a good boss holds off on answering phone calls and e-mails. This shows respect for your employees and demonstrates that you value their time and their contribution to your organization. If you are distracted and preoccupied with other things, the meeting is not productive, and the employee will feel unimportant.

Speak to your employees appropriately and respectfully, and make sure that you are as attentive to them as you expect them to be to you.

Leverages employee strengths and doesn't expose weaknesses

The more engaged you are with your staff, the more you will know about what they do well and where they shine. You'll also know any areas in which they may be limited. However, if those areas have no real impact on the employees' assigned duties, a good boss accepts those weaknesses and lets them go.

A client shared the story of an employee who once worked for him in an accounting position. The employee was uncomfortable being front and center in large groups; however, his former supervisor insisted that he deliver presentations as part of his duties. Although the information may have been exemplary, the employee's performance was always poor and undermined his confidence. As this man's new boss, my client took a different approach by delivering presentations himself, with the accountant alongside to address any points that needed elaborating. Rather than forcing a situation that didn't fit the employee's inherent personality, the client worked to accommodate, not expose, the "weakness."

Being the type of boss who does this will create a staff that trusts you and is eager to perform.

Understands that life exists outside work

I mentioned earlier how my husband, and partner in business, is known to walk around the office after 5 p.m. encouraging staff to pack it up and call it a day. A good boss understands that there is more to employees' lives than the work they perform.

Good bosses care as much about the people as they do the business running effectively and profitably. There will occasionally be unforeseen circumstances that interrupt your employees' work routine. Your willingness to accommodate the stumbling blocks will instill a sense of loyalty in your staff. They will not only appreciate you; they will also want to perform beyond expectations because you consider people first.

Knows that agility and flexibility lead to employee happiness and satisfaction

Consider a scenario where an excellent employee has to vacate his or her full-time position because of personal circumstances that prohibit the individual from maintaining his or her assigned schedule. The friend who picks up his or her child from school is moving, an elderly relative needs his or her help a couple of days per week, or any other situation that requires the employee's presence when he or she is normally at work. Instead of looking for a new hire, a truly good boss may want to evaluate that employee's job description. Can some of his or her work be done from home? Does the position truly require full-time hours, or can it be converted into a part-time job?

Many employers assume that part-time work means part-time effort. A good boss knows that isn't true. Don't rule out the possibility of part-time employees. More often than not, they will perform exceptionally well at their jobs because they are so appreciative of the opportunity to have balance between their personal and professional lives. They don't have as much stress about one area of their life interfering with the other.

Knows his or her own job

Your carefully crafted job descriptions and offer letters allow your employees to know precisely what is expected of them, and you keep up with performance evaluations to be sure everyone is on the same page. But what about your job description?

The boss must also meet criteria and fulfill expectations. Even if you're the top banana in the company, with no one above you to whom you report, it's imperative that you have a clearly defined role and that your employees see you fulfilling it.

If you want employees to stay on top of what you expect, set the example by showing that you know and respect your own responsibilities. I hear employees state, "I don't really know what he or she does" when speaking of managers. Don't let this be you.

Evaluates, doesn't judge

Never use performance evaluations to judge or criticize an employee. This most valuable tool should be used only as it is intended—to *evaluate* performance and determine how an employee can improve or grow in his or her job. Keep performance discussions professional while remaining aware of your employee's feelings. This is not the time to talk about specific incidents, which you should address when they occur.

Maintaining a policy of open communication can prevent misunderstandings, hurt feelings, and defensiveness at evaluation time. Be able to clearly express your reasons for the type of evaluation you are giving an employee. If you tell an employee he or she isn't ready to move to the next level, be able to tell him or her what the next level is and back up why you feel he or she isn't prepared for it yet. Otherwise, you're making a judgment about the employee's ability without giving him or her an assessment of what he or she needs to succeed.

Establishes a realistic workload and attainable goals

Every business has deadlines and goals to meet, and employees who are engaged and feel like a vital part of the company are glad to do their share to reach these goals. But setting unrealistic expectations for your staff won't get you to the result any faster; in fact, it just might derail productivity altogether.

Projects always have a target date, and a strong team works together to meet the deadline. It's your job to ensure that your teams aren't overburdened by excessive workloads and unattainable goals. As the manager, you must see the work is done with maximum efficiency, but that no one is crumbling under too much weight. A big project might occasionally require some overtime, but if your staff isn't leaving at their regular time because there's simply too much work to be done, you need to reevaluate the distribution of duties and find a way to alleviate some pressure.

Dumping a huge pile of work on an employee's desk on a Friday afternoon is a bad move. Even if the project isn't due until the following week, it creates a feeling of overload, especially for employees who like to end the week with a clear desk and start fresh on Monday. Assigning projects or tasks that are too much for employees to complete in a reasonable length of time is another sure-fire morale buster. When this type of project is finished, employees don't feel a sense of accomplishment or pride, just relief that the nightmare is over.

Setting realistic goals and workloads will help your employees feel motivated and energized. In a positive setting, they look forward to completing each step of a project, rather than seeing it as merely a hurdle to jump. Realistic expectations on your part go a long way toward fostering a sense of accomplishment and pride in your staff.

Asks, "What could I have done differently?"

Sometimes things go wrong, or at least, not quite as you planned. Nobody's perfect. The knee-jerk reaction is to place blame on something or someone else. Instead of being a jerk, a really good boss tries to figure out a better approach for next time and learn something from the situation. Whether a story about a project, a hiring, or a firing, every manager I spoke to relayed a scenario in which he or she asked this question to gain valuable insight to help make better decisions in the future.

Asks staff to evaluate him or her

This isn't easy. However, it is the most effective way I know to learn if you're on track for being the best boss you can be. Have your employees assess you as their boss.

Asking your staff to evaluate you as a manager will help you learn if you are coming up short and not doing 100 percent. The downside is that you may not like some of the feedback, assuming your staff is comfortable being honest with you. If they think you are going to be offended by any negative comments or take it out on them, the exercise will be pointless.

Should you decide to put yourself out there for evaluation, tell your staff they can do so anonymously. In a smaller office environment, you still may be able to determine who said what, so consider taking time to develop a form addressing various generic scenarios and have your employees rank you. Set up a system in which the way they submit the form can't be tracked back to them. Then take a deep breath, keep an open mind, pat yourself on the back about the things you do well, and work on the areas where you need improvement.

Their suggestions will benefit you as a manager, the employees you manage, and the company overall. Remember, do not get defensive. We respect and appreciate employees who embrace constructive criticism. It therefore stands to reason that employees will respect managers who embrace constrictive criticism.

Ten Signs You Could Be a Horrible Boss

According to the research I've done, most "bad bosses" did not know they were "bad." And in most cases, as soon as bosses become aware of their deficiencies, they seek out ways to improve.

If you recognize yourself in any of the signs below, make a commitment to change the behavior right now. Your employees—and your bottom line—will thank you.

1. You micromanage instead of manage.

Bad bosses try to tell their staff how to do their jobs. If you are spending more time on the small details and less time on the big picture, your employees probably don't like it.

2. You're engaged in office politics.

Don't be caught in the middle of office politics. If there are issues, have the employees work them out themselves or create forums to discuss solutions. Don't play favorites, pit employees against each other, or build alliances.

3. You bully and yell.

Bad bosses don't inspire; they bully and yell a lot. They try to get people to do things their way by threatening them with the loss of their job, verbally attacking them, or doing anything else other than making people feel and do their best. People who work in constant fear hate their job, their boss and the business. We don't like children to act this way so why would an adult be any different?

4. You have unclear objectives and motivations and send employees on wild goose races.

Never "test" an employee. It shows disrespect and is flat out an abuse of power and a waste of company time and money.

5. You don't give credit where it is due.

Great bosses love to recognize others' successes and achievements. Bad bosses are not only incapable of this, they also want to take the credit themselves. Andrew Carnegie said, "No man will make a great leader who wants to do it all himself, or to get all the credit for doing it."

6. You lack empathy and consideration.

If you think nothing of giving a ton of work to someone on Friday or you refuse to make accommodations to a schedule based on personal needs, this applies to you.

7. Your employees call in sick a lot.

This is a sure sign that they don't like work.

8. You rarely talk to your employees face-to-face.

Bad bosses avoid direct interaction with employees, and the majority of their correspondence is via e-mail, which can be very brief and impersonal.

9. You are inappropriate.

You touch too much, you curse, you tell offensive jokes, or you say inappropriate things.

10. You attack or talk badly about your team or your employees to friends, family, vendors and other managers.

What comes out of our mouths is a reflection of our thoughts and behaviors. If you do not respect your employees, they will know it.

Managing is not easy; if it were, organizational charts would be flat. I hope these suggestions will help you and others always strive to be the best that you can be!

Index

Book 1: Hire a Pro

Section 1

Section 2

CPSIA information can be obtained at www.ICGtesting.com
Printed in the USA
LVOW13193424051Z

28295JLV00003B/294/P

Be a Pro

The Job Seeker's Guide to Finding
the Right Job and Making Your
Employer Want to Keep You

Carey Baker

Owner, Part Time Pros

Published by Expert Message Group, LLC

Expert Message Group, LLC
P.O. Box 949
Tulsa, OK 74101

415.523.0404

www.expertmessagegroup.com

First Printing, April 2012

ISBN 978-1-936875-06-1

Printed in the United States of America
Set in Arno Pro 12.5/16.5

For permissions, please contact:
Expert Message Group, LLC
P.O. Box 949
Tulsa, OK 74101

I would like to dedicate this book to my husband Brett.
Brett has continued to be my champion, and has always encouraged
me to do more than I ever thought possible. Without his encouragement
and support this book would not be a reality.

About the author

Carey Baker began Part-Time Pros with her husband Brett Baker in 2008 after having her first daughter and realizing the need for flexibility in the corporate lifestyle. Part-Time Pros staffing company unites talented professionals with companies that have full- and part-time needs. The professionals range from stay-at-home moms wanting to contribute to their household income, to the early retirees looking to supplement retirement. The Tulsa-based company, which took second place in the 2009 Mayor's Entrepreneurial Spirit Award, works with more than 400 employer contracts and more than 6000 professionals. In 2011, Part-Time Pros was one of 75 businesses in the US to receive the US Chamber Blue Ribbon Award for growth and sustainability. In her free time, Carey loves date nights with her husband Brett, cross fit, and rough housing with her girls. The Bakers live in Tulsa, Oklahoma with their two daughters Kennedy and Gentry. Carey is available to speak to your organization or association, call (918) 551-7767 for booking.

Contents

How to Use This Book

The book you are holding offers a unique opportunity to learn the ins and outs of finding and keeping a great job. You'll find tips on maximizing your job search, submitting a résumé, and preparing for interviews. There is also information on things to consider before accepting an offer and how to make your new boss want to keep you on the payroll for years to come.

What is different about this book is that it gives you the added perspective of learning what hiring managers expect when they post a position and interview applicants. You'll also learn first-hand how to take the anxiety out of a performance appraisal by understanding how to communicate with your boss.

Helpful information is delivered in easy-to-follow sections, with examples of real-world scenarios to illustrate important points. You can read the book straight through for a comprehensive overview, but each section stands on its own to help you find the specific information you need. Want to write a killer cover letter that's sure to get your résumé noticed? Check out the index and go directly to the section you're looking for.

If you'd like some additional insight into how employers think, flip the book over. The other half is written for hiring professionals, but it's sure to give you lots of food for thought. Scanning that information will add to your understanding of your current boss, and give you some great ideas for making the most of your job.

Introduction

When you're looking for a job, you're careful to update your résumé and ensure you present yourself in the best possible light to each prospective employer. You make sure your references are up to date, your interview attire is appropriate, and you are on time for your appointment. Before you leave for your interview, however, there's another item to check off your list that will put you ahead in the running for a potential job.

One of the strongest tools in a job seeker's arsenal is the ability to consider exactly what an employer will expect of you. You will score points in an interview by displaying an understanding that the company has specific needs to fill. Employers appreciate candidates who have done their homework and show that they are serious about the position.

It might sound surprising, but one of the first things a company needs you to be certain about is what your own priorities are. It's up to you to be clear about what you need and want from your next position.

To find the job that will be the right fit, you have to take the time to think carefully about what you really want. You must recognize your own needs before you start applying for jobs. This will streamline your job search because you'll only be looking at companies that meet your criteria; it will also help you determine right away whether a job offer is the right one for you to accept. On the flip side, your clarity will save prospective employers time by focusing on your precise needs and skills, something that all companies appreciate.

Think about whether you want to spend all of your hours in an office or

would prefer to telecommute. Be clear about the salary you require so you will apply for or accept interviews only for positions that meet your needs. Perhaps you are interested in working part-time or on a flexible schedule. In that case, determining exactly the days and hours you can work each week is especially important.

Although finding a job may be imperative, being desperate for work will get you nowhere. Companies can see this and will think that you will settle for anything until something better comes along; they won't be willing to invest the time and money to train you. Most companies also view short tenure with three or more companies in a row as a major red flag (some companies even go as far as disqualifying job hoppers). I hope that young graduates in particular are aware of this, because job-hopping can drastically affect your career path if you are not careful.

A friend of mine who is 40 years old and has a master's degree is now stuck in retail sales because she hopped from job to job. She has asked me why she can't get hired by a great company, and I've told her it's because she stays with an employer for only a year and then leaves. Her work history has now drastically limited who will even consider her for employment.

Think about your work history and consider how happy you've been in different jobs. You'll find that those where you were most satisfied are those where you felt the most comfortable. It might sound simple, but too many people don't give it enough thought. Are you more comfortable working closely with colleagues, or do you prefer the quiet of your own office? Do you want to work in a formal corporate culture or a more relaxed, informal atmosphere? You already know the answers; don't overlook their significance. Being honest with yourself is the most important thing you can do to ensure your happiness on the job.

In addition to what you want from a job, don't forget to get specific about what you can offer. Know what you are good at and apply only to positions that are a good fit with your skills. This shows a level of professionalism that will be appreciated by hiring managers, because you won't be wasting their time.

Just as you have your needs and preferences, every company you apply

to will have its own particular mission and values. You'll do yourself (as well as your prospective employer) a favor by learning what those are and acknowledging whether you can commit to them.

This might sound a bit strange, but when you are considering a new job, it's good to remember that actually, it's not all about you. A company is only as good as the employees who work for it, and the company stands to gain or lose a lot by investing in you. You've got to be willing and able to become part of the team that makes the company successful. The way to do that is to be honest and committed, to consciously work at creating a positive experience for yourself and your employer.

In addition to knowing your own needs, think carefully about how your individual skills will be an asset to the company. This will prepare you with confidence, not only for the interview process but also in your quest to be an employee who exceeds expectations.

SECTION 1
Maximize Your Job Search

Searching for a new job can be a time of real stress, especially in a highly competitive job market. With record numbers of Americans unemployed, hiring professionals receive hundreds upon hundreds of applications for every available position. Yet there's a way to make yours stand out and be noticed.

Step 1: Know what you're good at

The first step toward finding the job that's the right fit for you begins with one word: Honesty.

The very best thing you can do to make your job search efficient and effective is to be honest with yourself about your skills and abilities. Think very specifically about what you're good at. Saying "I'm a receptionist" isn't enough. Are you a receptionist with the skills to manage a complex communications system for a large company while greeting visitors and attending to paperwork, or is your experience limited to smaller, less formal offices? The difference is huge. Listing "proficient in Microsoft Office" on your

résumé doesn't mean much if you're good only at Word and can't produce a complex Excel document. Nail down your provable skills; if you're granted an interview, you can express a willingness to learn others.

Knowing what you are good at will also help focus your job search. You know that looking for work is time-consuming. Researching listings, writing cover letters, completing applications—all require a lot of your attention. On the flip side, the people to whom you're applying are equally pressed for time, often having to review an overwhelming number of applications.

If you know what you're good at and apply only to positions that you're a good fit for, you'll save time by narrowing your search. Applying for only those positions that you are truly qualified for also shows a level of professionalism. Hiring managers appreciate that you have taken the time to consider whether the job is a match for your skills. If a company has more than one position available and your résumé appears in response to all of them, that's a red flag; it indicates that you haven't fully addressed either the company's needs or your ability to fill them. Hiring managers also find it frustrating when a person applies to jobs for which he or she has no experience.

I have actually heard of companies banning applicants because they apply for every open position, regardless of whether they have the right skills. Don't be this person! On the other hand, if it's a company that you really want to work for, you can still submit a résumé, but do so carefully. Write a cover letter, addressed to the hiring manager or HR director, explaining your purpose:

"Dear X:

Although I do not have the skills necessary for this job, I do possess the following skills: (list out). Should you have any open positions in the future that I would be a fit for or know of a company that could use my expertise, I would appreciate your consideration. Thank you in advance for the time you took to review my résumé."

This shows initiative and confidence, and indicates a level of professionalism that may well keep you in mind for a future position.

Step 2: Your résumé

For this second step of your process, we're going to continue with the theme of honesty. I recently read a statistic that floored me, despite all of my experience as a hiring professional. It has been estimated that seventy-three percent of all résumés contain false information or some embellishment of the truth. The reason I was so surprised is not because people lie; it's because they are willing to take a risk by lying about something so very important.

Your résumé is your passport to the land of your next job; it's generally the employer's first impression of you. Why chance misrepresenting your abilities at this crucial first step? Be honest about your skills and experience. Looking for a job can be stressful enough without worrying about being caught in a lie or being asked to prove a skill that you're not really proficient at.

While we're on the subject, it's worth mentioning that not every false résumé exaggerates an applicant's abilities. Particularly when times are tough, people are often tempted to "dumb down" their résumés so they don't appear overqualified for jobs. I advise against this as well. If you claim to have worked as an account representative rather than as director of marketing, a check with your previous employer will reveal the truth. Better to be honest and explain why you are interested in a lower-level position, a strategy that just might make a prospective employer see the value of your experience.

There are two main résumé formats that I see every day. One is the functional résumé, which lists a person's skills and strengths, followed by his or her work history. The other is the chronological résumé, which shows an applicant's work history right off. I much prefer this to the functional style, which wastes my time by making me search for the pertinent information I need. Prepare a chronological résumé, which is clear and concise and allows you to be very specific about what you have accomplished, where you have worked, and how long you worked there.

Be specific in your résumé. A vague résumé that doesn't tell the hiring professional anything concrete about your skills and experience won't get noticed. Think carefully about what you have done at all of your jobs, and translate those tasks into concise bullets that express accomplishments and demonstrate responsibility. Your goal is to make those accomplishments jump out at the person reading the résumé.

Look carefully at your résumé each time you submit it to be sure it is targeted to the specific position you are applying for. Too many people make the mistake of thinking that one résumé is sufficient for all their needs. That's not the case. Depending on the job description, you might want to stress certain work experience or skills over others to highlight your strengths for that position.

Have two or three people read your résumé and summarize verbally and in writing what "type" of job they think you would be good at. Chances are their interpretations will mirror those of hiring managers. Don't get defensive if you are offered suggestions; listen to the suggestions and take them to heart. All too often, I have had conversations with applicants who state, "I can do this job." However, that is not clear to me when I look at their résumé. Make sure your résumé accurately reflects your skills. Just because it makes sense to you does not mean it makes sense to a stranger who knows nothing about you and what skills you bring to the table. Here is a challenge I would like to present you, show your finished résumé to at least one stranger. Give them 5 seconds to review your résumé and then ask them what they think you would be good at.

If you are uncertain about how to prepare an effective résumé, there are lots of books and online resources you can consult for advice.

Step 3: Your cover letter

The best résumé in the world won't get you hired if an employer doesn't even see it. There's one main reason a potential employer wouldn't see it, and that's if it's introduced by a boring cover letter.

Here is some first-hand advice from an employer who has read one too many bad cover letters and wants to help you avoid the trap.

Tips Directly from the Source on How to Apply for a Job

The following funny and true posting appeared on Craigslist after the CEO of a company decided to enlighten applicants on how to best get his—or other potential employers'—attention.

Dear prospective job hunters,

Thank you for taking the time to look at our site, and thank you for being interested in working with us.

Most applications I receive go straight to the deleted-items folder because of a few simple mistakes. I'm beginning to feel bad, so if you are going to make the effort to apply for a job here, or anywhere else, I'd like to offer you some advice.

To successfully interest me in hiring you, you need to understand what we as business owners face on the other side of the fence. Hiring is the most important task I face, but it is also 76th on my list of 100 other things to do today. When we put a posting on Craigslist, we usually get around 100 responses within 48 hours. They flood into my inbox, and I have to push them aside until I have time to give them the attention they deserve. In the meantime, I have phones ringing, deadlines to meet, problems with our systems, employees with questions, and much more to compete for the limited capacity of my brain.

But don't let this put you off. It doesn't take much to distinguish yourself. Here's how:

1. YOUR COVER LETTER MUST ANSWER OUR NEEDS.

When I do get round to your e-mail, I do not have time to look at every detail. I make quick and rapid decisions about whether I will call you or not. I don't even get to most résumés because the cover letter is so drab. If you want to stand a chance at getting a response, you ABSOLUTELY MUST spend some time on this.

So, how should you write a cover letter? Simple, read our post, and tell me quickly how you can meet the needs we have listed. Use examples wherever possible. Take a look at these two different letters:

An excellent cover letter (5 percent are like this)

James,

OK, I admit. I saw your posting just now for the Product Marketing Manager for Outdoor Adventures and Experiences just now on Craigslist, and I'm salivating. I can't imagine a better adventure for a career than to market excitement and fun. Let me tell you three reasons you should consider me for this position:

Strong design skills - Your ad said you were looking for someone who can design brochures and other marketing materials. I have two years of design experience, and am proficient in Adobe Illustrator and Pagemaker. I have created brochures for XYZ company and ABC company, and have attached a PDF of my work. I'd be happy to show you my portfolio in an interview.

Good communication and writing skills - In my former job, I regularly led meetings that involved dozens of people. Several times a year, I would speak for my company at industry events … sometimes to audiences of several hundred people. I know how to craft a good press release and have managed to get several articles into print.

I love experiences - I completely relate to your philosophy that life is about experiences. I love to travel, and have recently returned from two months in Peru where I helped feed orphan children in a small town. I've never been skydiving, but it is on my top ten list of things to do next year. Perhaps this is my opportunity.

Experience -THIS is a place where I know I can make a difference, and with my experience in conceiving plans and putting projects

into motion, I'm sure I could impact your company very quickly without spending too much time in the starting gate. I would love to meet with you in person to talk about how I can help take the adventure to a whole new level.

The run-of-the-mill cover letter (95 percent are exactly the same)

Dear Sir/Madam:

Please accept this letter and resume for the Product Marketing Manager position as referenced on craigslist.com.

As a recent MBA graduate, I believe that I offer the skills that are crucial to this position. My background in marketing, as well as my formal education in business and marketing from UCLA, will serve as a complement to your firm.

After doing some extensive research about experienceTHIS. us, I am sure that my work history and educational background will greatly benefit the future endeavors of your organization. (Did you really do extensive research on us??? - no evidence here, that's for sure.) My work history coupled with my education in business administration has provided me with an invaluable sense of communication and negotiation, as well as quantitative analytical skills. Blah Blah Blah

From both my professional and personal experiences, I have developed an enthusiastic, entrepreneurial, and disciplined work ethic. I possess the ability to work under pressure and rapidly adapt to changing work conditions. I excel in both individual- and team-driven environments. With this in mind, I am confident that my employment background, eagerness to learn, and genuine character will prove to be an asset to your company. Blah Blah Blah

I look forward to discussing employment opportunities with you in the near future. I am available for an interview at your earliest

convenience. Thank you in advance for your consideration. Blah Blah Blah

Which one would you call?

The run-of-the-mill one doesn't even come close to responding to what we're looking for. If you just regurgitate a form cover letter from some book you read, or the e-mail you sent to the last company, I'm going to yawn and hit the delete key before I ever get to your resume. I feel bad doing it, but I just don't have time for blah blah blah.

2. Don't blah blah blah.

Be super clear and concise. Use the same language to describe your achievements to me, as you would to your grandmother. For example ...

"My work history coupled with my education in business administration has provided me with an invaluable sense of communication and negotiation, as well as quantitative analytical skills."

Yawn. This means nothing to me. Compare it to this ...

"I have had really only one job. It was at Larry's Video Store near my college. We were losing customers to Netflix, so I helped persuade my boss to offer a subscription service to our customers. I made up a business model of our projected sales, and showed how this would improve our bottom line. My boss agreed, and told me to spread the word. I designed flyers and put up posters around campus to promote our new service. Our subscription model was a success, and I'm sure my boss Larry would sing my praises for my business and marketing initiative."

Be clear, concise, and factual. Don't use fluffy words. Describe yourself, who you are, and how exactly you can help. If you

can't make a selling proposition for yourself, how on earth will you do it for me?

3. Don't make the mistake of attaching your cover letter as a Word document.

You're writing me an e-mail. Imagine me sitting at my desk with my inbox dinging every minute. Do you think I really want to fire up Word to see a formatted cover letter? No. Just write your cover letter as you would any other e-mail. That's what e-mail is for.

4. Respond with the title of the job advertisement in the subject heading.

Yes, it's good to use some initiative in the subject line to grab my attention, but I sort my e-mail based on subject, and if you're not in the right subject, you're going to get lost.

Bad: I love skydiving and work really hard

Good: Product Manager job

Best: Product Manager job (I love skydiving and work really hard)

5. Win me over by being open and honest.

I respect failure, and I look for potential. Yet it seems to be common practice to BS on résumés nowadays. It's okay to be proud of your accomplishments, but a little modesty makes you look human. I'd much rather meet with someone who admits he's failed than someone who pretends he's always been successful.

"I successfully led a ten-person team to generate sales of $200,000."

Yeah, okay … but I'd respect that person even more if she had the guts to write this:

"In my last job, I had ten people working for me. It was stressful, and I didn't have a clue about how to manage at the time. Two of my team resigned in the first month, and I found it difficult to motivate the other eight who were all older than me. We still met our quota, but I was let go. To be fair, I was in over my head at the time. I have since been to two leadership training seminars, and I can see now where I went wrong."

Which one would you rather talk to?

Must get back to work now, but I hope this has helped you out.

James Dilworth, CEO experienceTHIS.us - Experiences make better gifts

P.S. We're still looking for a Product Manager.

P.P.S. I found a reply this morning from someone with a different perspective. If you're applying to an accounting job with a large corporation, where the HR manager lets dust collect on her bifocals, you may not want to heed all of my advice.

Step 4: The interview

Once you've been invited for an interview, it's time to begin the next phase of your preparation. Here's a great tip to give you an advantage: ask the person who contacts you if you can see a copy of the job description before the interview. This will help you prepare for questions about the specifics of the job; you can also formulate any questions you may have about the position.

Of course, you'll be asked about your skills and experience, but a savvy interviewer will use the time to learn more about you than what is easily gleaned from your résumé and application.

Make a good impression right off the bat by avoiding these unprofessional behaviors:

- Showing up late for an interview and acting as if everything is fine.

- Forgetting about an interview.

- Booking too many interviews in the same time frame.

- Arriving at an interview without a résumé.

- Being poorly dressed or groomed. Even if a company is "business casual," you should dress smartly during the interviewing process.

- Not showing enthusiasm for the position for which you are interviewing.

- Expressing interest in positions other than the one for which you are interviewing.

- Stalker calling recruiters/hiring managers. Don't confuse being persistent with stalking. If a recruiter says he or she will get back to you next week, wait until he or she gets back to you next week. Calling and e-mailing every day will not get you a job or an interview; in fact, it may take you from the "maybe" file to the trash.

- Talking negatively about former employers. I take that back. Any negative talk during an interview is not appropriate. In fact, try to avoid any negativity at the office if at all possible. Your managers will appreciate this.

- Leaving a voicemail without including your name and callback number.

- Receiving a voicemail and returning the call without listening to the message. Don't call back and say, "Someone from this number called me." There may be a dozen people in the office who could have called you; you can't expect the display number to show a direct line.

- Sending an e-mail without a signature.

- Talking on your cell phone or using electronic devices while waiting for an interview to start.

- Answering text messages or phone calls during an interview.

- Not accepting an offer because you want more money. You should not have applied for the position if it did not meet your salary requirements.

- Not accepting an offer because you are better off on unemployment. If the salary laid out in the job description did not meet or exceed your needs, you should not have applied for the job.

Remember that the employer is trying to find the person who fits best with the company's culture and core values, and the interview is a good way to determine whether you will complement those values. For example, if a company places a high premium on integrity, you might be asked for an example of a situation in which you exhibited that trait. If efficiency is important, the interviewer might ask you to describe a situation when your efficiency made a positive difference.

If you are unprepared for questions such as these, you'll be caught off guard and will seem less confident. Take some time before your interview to think about traits and characteristics aside from your measurable skills. If you've already compiled your list of what you want or need from a job, this won't be difficult. For instance, if personal fulfillment is important to you, you should be able to talk comfortably about how you handle the work/life balance. Have a few examples ready that illustrate your strengths. Even if you aren't asked specifically to discuss these things, you can bring them up when the interviewer asks if there's anything else you'd like to add.

Here are the types of questions you should be prepared to answer:

- Why did you get into this line of work?

- What will a company gain by hiring you?

- What are your strengths?

- What are your weaknesses?

- What is one of the toughest problems you've ever solved?

These are fairly straightforward questions that almost any interviewer will ask a potential employee. You should not be rattled by them. A more creative hiring manager might try to get you to think outside the box by

asking questions you may not expect that will help the interviewer judge whether your values fit with those of the company.

A couple of questions along these lines might be:

- Would you tell your boss that a coworker told you he submitted phony expenses on his expense reimbursement sheet?

- If we hire you, what is the most important thing you'll do on your first day of work?

- What do you know about our company?

There's one moment in an interview I know a lot of people dread. It's when you're asked if you have any questions. An interview should be a two-way street, and you *should* ask questions. Just as the hiring manager needs to learn about you, you are perfectly entitled to learn more about the job and the company, too. A willingness to answer your questions also tells you a lot about the potential employer's level of respect for his or her employees. You can show a level of professionalism by using the interview to ask for specifics that will help you know if this is, indeed, the right job for you, without wasting anyone's time.

Suggested questions:

- What are the major responsibilities of this position?

- What are the biggest challenges in this position?

- Who does this position report to?

- Tell me about his or her management style or what type of person works best for that individual.

- Has the budget for the team/department been increasing or decreasing?

- What is the company culture like?

- What happened to the person who previously held this position?

- Are there any drawbacks to this position?

- What types of projects will this team or position be handling in the future?

- Where do you see the company headed in the next five years?

At the close of the interview, ask, "Do you think I might be a fit?" If answered honestly, this question will help you see whether you are a good match for the company. It accomplishes a few important things:

By putting the question in the third person, you are not asking what the interviewer thinks of you personally, but instead what he or she thinks of your skills and of the potential "fit."

The answer may be "good," or it may tell you that something is missing that you might have a chance to address.

Don't be defensive if the answer isn't 100 percent positive. Keep your ears open because the interviewer may be giving you great feedback for future job interviews or allowing you a chance to clarify a miscommunication. There is no such thing as a perfect candidate, and it is normal for interviewers to have some concerns.

Asking how the interviewer sees the fit gives you a chance to address additional items that may not have come up in the interview.

Always thank the interviewer for his or her time and tell him or her that you look forward to the possibility of working with him or her.

If these topics haven't come up during the interview, it's perfectly appropriate to ask about the work schedule and training policies. It's even acceptable to ask about the dress code, since this will give you a sense of the company's culture and help you decide whether you'll fit in. If it's a suit-and-tie office and your wardrobe consists of casual Friday attire, you might want to rethink things.

You can ask what the average tenure is in positions similar to the one you are applying for. Employees stay at jobs because of good managers and good coworkers, so asking this question will give you a sense of whether the work environment is positive.

There's one question that will give you terrific insight into what the company is looking for. Ask the interviewer, "If you could share with me

the attributes of your best employee, what qualities would he or she have?" Consider the answer carefully to see if you have the qualities the interviewer is looking for.

One topic that doesn't generally come up in an interview is the potential for growth. It's not appropriate to ask, "Where can I go from here?" before you've even been hired. However, if the interviewer broaches the subject, answer honestly. I tell potential employees about the possibilities for growth right up front. In fact, when I laid out the growth potential for one applicant and asked if he thought he would be happy in the job and stay with us, he responded that he would not. I thanked him for his honesty and hired someone else. We both saved time; nothing was lost.

If the interview was conducted well, you and the hiring manager should have ample information to determine whether you are the best candidate for the job. You should come away knowing if this is a company where you want to work.

Here's a bit of advice for making a guaranteed positive impression. Immediately following your interview, write a handwritten note to the person who interviewed you, thanking him or her for his or her time and restating your interest and availability. Make sure to double-check your spelling! This common courtesy has become so infrequent that it will set you apart.

Step 5: References

Your interview was a success, and the hiring manager has asked for your references. He or she will contact your previous employer to verify facts, such as your job title and dates of employment. Beyond that information, your prospective employer will want to know about other factors that will contribute to the hiring decision.

Some employers like to contact former coworkers as well, to get a sense of how you fit in the office dynamic and worked with a team. If you held a supervisory position, some of your past employees might be asked about your management style.

All of this information contributes to the employer's overall view of you as an employee and as a person. Even if your references stick to the facts of

your former job, the answers to these questions will help your prospective employer gain insight into your personality and work ethic.

Many companies, particularly large organizations, follow a policy of verifying employment only, which means your prospective employer might get no further than the HR department at your former job. It may also mean that your prospective employer won't get the opportunity to speak with the people who can attest to your strengths and potential. There is a way to overcome this roadblock, though. You can personally ask past managers or coworkers to write letters on your behalf which you can present as references. In this way, they are endorsing you personally, not on behalf of the company. This shows a positive, proactive attitude that should make a good impression on a future employer.

Here are some questions you might ask employers and colleagues to address in a letter of reference:

- What strengths did I exhibit?

- How did I show growth and improvement?

- Did I work with integrity and ethics?

- How did I function as part of a team?

- Were my skills appropriate for the job I was assigned to do?

- Did I take initiative and responsibility?

- Can you describe any particular achievement that was noteworthy?

Make sure your references know that you are providing their names, and be sure you are 100 percent confident about what they will say about you. Verify that you have the right phone numbers and e-mail addresses (if you don't have their appropriate contact information, should they really be a reference?).

If you are competing with another candidate who has skills and abilities equal to yours but whose references come back more quickly than yours, you may not get an offer simply because some managers assume

a delayed response is an indication of poor performance or that you are hiding something.

There is something else you can do to enhance the reference search. Most employers take advantage of social media to get a sense of a prospective employee. I know I do. Don't put anything out there that you wouldn't want your new boss to see. If you need to complain about work, do it privately, not on your Facebook page. I would think twice about hiring someone who is willing to post negative or questionable material. Set your privacy setting to display information only to friends or connections. Employers want employees who can leave their personal lives, problems, and issues at home, not someone who brings drama to the workplace. You have to remember that a medium like Facebook is for more than sharing video clips with your friends. Don't let it end up working against you in your job search.

These are the steps you should follow to conduct an efficient and successful job search. Staying honest with yourself will affect each step, making the next one that much easier. Maintaining your professionalism throughout the process will shine through to potential employers, and will keep you focused on your goal. In addition, if your professionalism does not result in a job offer, it may result in a referral to another potential job.

A Word of Caution: Don't Jump at a Job Offer

You aced your interview, and all of your references were glowing. Congratulations, you've received a job offer!

This, of course, is excellent news. However, before you jump right in and accept the offer, you should carefully consider whether you are really making the best decision. No amount of research and preparation is too much when it comes to something as important as accepting a job offer. Get back to the person who has extended the offer and ask them if you can have a day to talk it over with loved ones or think about it. Tell them that you are truly excited about the opportunity but that you like to give every big decision thought.

Be sure you can deliver

When you prepared your résumé to specifically address the job in question, and when you carefully considered your answers and questions for the interview, you were essentially selling your skills and knowledge to the employer.

Now that you've received an offer, you have to consider whether you are truly able and ready to make good on the sale and perform in the way you've indicated. Again, it comes down to honesty. It's worth taking the time to think about each assertion you've made to the employer about your abilities. Can you fulfill them?

Starting a new job is not the time to exaggerate your credentials. I hope that you haven't done so, because you'll have to live up to the expectations you've set. If you have been honest throughout the application process, you shouldn't worry. Just be sure that your skills are sharp and that you are prepared to deliver on what you've promised.

Explore the company culture

Though this was addressed earlier, it bears reiterating here. The culture of the company extending the job offer should be a primary consideration before you accept a position. No degree of skill or experience will make you happy if the company is simply the wrong fit for you.

If you haven't already done so, research the company. Find all the information you can about its mission, values, and style. Know whether you can fit into and uphold the company's culture. During the time since your interview, additional questions may have occurred to you; it's okay to ask them before you accept an offer. Just be sure to cover all the important bases. Know your criteria and get the answers you need.

Make a commitment

Once you have your answers and believe the job is the right choice, be prepared to make a full commitment. As carefully as you are evaluating the company that's offered you a job, that's how carefully the hiring manager

has weighed your credentials against the company's needs. Your resume has been considered, time has been devoted to at least one, probably two interviews, and your references have been contacted. After that investment of time, the employer is ready to commit to hiring you.

It is up to you—in fact, it is your responsibility—to make a commitment in turn. You should also realize that you are not only making a commitment to the employer; you are also making a commitment to yourself. You are committing to deliver on what you've offered in terms of skills and experience, to do the best possible job that you can to enhance—and advance—your professional and personal development.

You never know where a job might lead you. By committing to do your absolute best in this position, you might be taking the first step toward growth within the company or an excellent reference down the road.

Lack of commitment could end up costing you more than you think. If you accept a position ambivalently, thinking that if it doesn't work out you'll just bide your time until the job you really want comes along, you may find yourself bouncing from job to job. A few months here, a year there, doesn't reflect well on a candidate's resume. Potential employers have nothing to go on but your track record. You may be better off not accepting an offer than portraying yourself as irresponsible and unreliable.

You are an investment

In addition to the time spent on interviewing and checking your references, the job offer implies a substantial financial investment in you. For the employer, hiring a new employee represents a good deal more than the amount of your weekly paycheck. Here is a breakdown of what a company actually pays out each year for an employee earning $40,000:

Cost to employ a person for one year paying him or her a $40,000 salary
- Four major mandatory employer-paid payroll taxes

    - Social Security: 6.2 percent

    - Medicare: 1.45 percent

- Federal Unemployment Rate (FUTA): 6.2 percent up to $7,000 of salary

- State Unemployment (SUTA): varies by state and employer: Part-Time Pros pays 2.7 percent

- Workman's Comp Insurance: 0.8 percent

- Optional costs

    - 401(k) matching

    - Medical insurance

    - Paid vacation

    - Sick days

Various articles have stated that hiring an employee costs the employer 25 percent to 40 percent above the annual salary. A $40,000 employee costs the employer at least $50,000 and as much as $56,000.

This financial scenario should help you understand why companies must be highly selective when filling jobs, and why you must be sure you are making the right decision when you accept an offer. When you take on a new job, you and your employer are making an investment, one that merits thorough research and careful consideration.

SECTION 2
How to Be a Pro

When you start a new job, your objective should be to become a superstar employee. You want to be an addition to the company your employer will never regret hiring, someone the company will want to keep as part of the team because of your exemplary performance.

A superstar exceeds his or her employer's expectations, and makes the employer proud of how the employee represents the company. A superstar excels to the point that the boss would have no qualms about putting him or her on national television to speak about the business, because the employee exudes the values the company holds true.

It might surprise you that you should take the first step toward becoming a superstar *before* you're even hired. Sound impossible? Not at all. One of my own superstars impressed me during her interview when *she interviewed me* to get answers to questions that were important in making her job decision.

For instance, as a mom with young children, she was concerned about how our company handles time off for holidays and whether she would be able to work from home on occasion. Since these issues are a big part of the Part-Time Pros culture, I knew, on this front at least, she would be a good fit. However, in addition, I was extremely pleased that she took the initiative

to broach her concerns. Her timing was also perfect. She did not throw it out during the first interview that a work/life balance was a big priority to her. Rather, she waited until the second interview, when she knew I was interested in her and that she was interested in our company. The timing was appropriate because I had asked her about any questions or concerns she might have, which gave her the opening to broach the subject.

She also asked if she could speak to the employee she would be replacing as well as at least one other member of my staff, which I think is a terrific question. What better way to learn how it would be to work for me than to hear it directly from the source? This showed me that she was serious about determining whether this job would be right for her, and told me that she wasn't about to settle for any job just for the sake of taking it. In fact, today this employee says that this is the most satisfied she's ever felt in a job, which is tremendously rewarding for me.

If there are issues that will be a big factor in your decision-making process, don't hesitate to bring them up during your interview. The employer would much rather know your concerns at the outset than find out about them after you've been hired.

Once you are hired, you want to do all you can to make a company do everything it possibly can to keep you. You want to Be a Pro.

Step 1: Balance

My superstar employee asked a very insightful question during her interview. Since staffing can be an extremely busy, sometimes almost round-the-clock business, she asked how I "turn it off." This is an excellent question. It does not imply that a candidate is looking for a way to get around working hard; it shows that the person is concerned about maintaining a healthy balance between work and his or her personal life. And she knew that my answer would be indicative of the company's culture.

My own philosophy is that there is nothing so important that it warrants working until midnight. I appreciate every minute that my employees devote to their jobs, but I don't expect them to sacrifice their lives for work. I want them to go home when their shift is over, because I know that having

a healthy work/life balance keeps them refreshed and energized.

Burnout is the bane of employees and employers. You never want to reach the point when you simply dread doing the same job every day. Your employer never wants to see you reach that point either, because it's unhealthy for you and the company. Everyone needs a break from the typical routine once in a while, and staying aware of your work/life balance helps provide some variety and avoid burnout.

You know what types of interests and activities you enjoy in your personal life; these can actually benefit you in your job as well, so be sure to make room for them in your schedule. If you give up doing something you love, like working out or playing a sport, because you're too busy with your work, you'll resent your job and your employer. You won't perform well, and nobody wins.

You can also pursue interests that will help boost your level of satisfaction at work. For instance, you might consider some continuing education courses or training, perhaps working toward a certification in your field. This gives you things to do outside work that keep you fulfilled. You're still focusing on work, but in a fresh setting. This can be especially important in an industry where many jobs require workers to perform repetitive tasks, such as manufacturing, where burnout is a real danger.

Whatever your industry, you should be able to find opportunities to expand your horizons and bring some variety into your routine. One of my employees volunteers at a job transition ministry established by a local church. Once or twice a month, she helps people who are out of work by reviewing résumés, conducting mock interviews, and giving presentations. She feels a real sense of fulfillment that shows in her positive attitude at work. In fact, her volunteering led to our company placing an applicant from the ministry in a high-level position. A win-win for sure.

Step 2: Efficiency

As a business owner, I need my employees to perform as efficiently as possible. That is paramount to the company's success and, ultimately, to their own fulfillment. The team as a whole benefits when each member works at maximum efficiency.

A superstar employee makes efficiency a top priority. Complete a task before moving on to the next one. Maintain a neat and organized workspace; if your boss or a coworker has to look for something while you are away from your desk, he or she won't waste time going through paperwork that should have been filed last week. Be able to back up your decisions and actions, so if your employer needs clarification on something, you'll have the answer at hand.

Uncertain expectations are a deterrent to efficiency. If you are at all unsure about what it is expected of you, waste no time asking for clarification. Your job description should clearly lay out your responsibilities, but if you have a question, ask.

Working efficiently is a clear indicator that your employer can trust you, which is vital to a company's success. Without trust, my company couldn't move forward because I'd be mired in the morass of double-checking everyone's work and wouldn't have sufficient time for my own responsibilities.

Granted, building trust happens over time, and even the most promising new hires have to prove themselves by doing their job accurately and efficiently until the employer is confident in their abilities. So don't get upset or put off if your new employer doesn't immediately recognize you for the superstar you are. Give your employer the chance to see you shine by observing you. He or she needs and wants to trust you with your job so that you can perform efficiently and effectively. No one likes someone looking over his or her shoulder, but by the same token, superstar employees recognize they need to prove themselves to gain their employer's trust.

Step 3: Accountability

One of the surest signs of a superstar employee is a high level of accountability. From minor details to major responsibilities, this is one area where you can never do too much.

You are accountable for successfully and efficiently completing every task assigned to you. There might well be a thing or two about your job that aren't your favorites, but they deserve no less attention than the things that put a smile on your face. Like 'em or not, the items in your job description add up

to the entire picture; slacking on one will only make less of the whole.

Even the best employee is going to receive negative feedback at some point, and the way you handle it can make or break your road to superstardom. A stellar employee handles feedback, and even a discussion about a performance issue, calmly and professionally, never defensively. Recognize negative feedback from your boss as constructive, and use it to improve your performance. If you are called out on a performance issue, again, don't be defensive. Listen to what your employer has to say; if you disagree, state your case calmly and clearly. However, if you see the boss's point, be accountable, and own up to the issue at hand, and ask how you can correct it.

There are so many ways you can be accountable. For example, be respectful of everyone's work time. You know what time you're expected at work; it's your responsibility to show up on time. If the bus schedule gets you to work ten minutes late, take an earlier bus. Don't expect the rest of the team to carry you, even for ten minutes. It causes resentment because it shows a lack of respect. Doing your part to get to work on time shows a high level of respect for everyone on the team.

Employers and employees alike have lives outside the workplace, and all of those lives may occasionally get a bit messy. A true professional is aware of this fact but doesn't bring drama to the workplace. If you work in a congenial environment, it's perfectly normal for coworkers to inquire about one another's families and circumstances. People might be aware that you have a difficult situation, such as an ill parent or marital problems, and talking about it briefly is okay. Just don't allow your problems to distract everyone else.

You should not allow any personal problems to interfere with your own work, either. If a situation becomes so severe that you are unable to do your job, talk with your employer about scheduling some time off to deal with it. Although you might think it better to soldier through, your boss is more likely to appreciate your honesty and the fact that you don't want your personal situation to interfere with your work or affect others performance.

Life happens. Children are going to get sick, medical appointments are going to be made that interfere with traditional work hours. In some work environments, working from home occasionally can make up for

time missed in the office. The point is that you have to be accountable for that balance. For example, I don't mind if someone in my company has to leave early to attend a parent–teacher conference, but I do expect that appointment to be on the calendar. I don't want to look for that person and be unaware he or she isn't in the office.

To be a superstar, be accountable not only for what's listed in your job description but also for your contribution to the team.

Step 4: Professionalism

Simply stated, it is impossible to become a superstar employee without exhibiting a high level of professionalism. This is one quality that you can begin to show as early as when you apply for a job. Presenting an error-free résumé and application, being courteous to the receptionist and staff, being on time and appropriately dressed for an interview, formally thanking the person who took the time to interview you—these are all professional behaviors that make an impression on a prospective employer.

It doesn't matter what industry you work in; every job has standards to be met, and the degree to which you meet them says a lot about whether you're cut out to be a superstar.

I've talked about the need to understand a company's culture, but it really is so important that it bears repeating. Know what your company values in an employee, what will make you fit in and stand out. When you embrace those qualities and make them part of your professional demeanor, your employer can't help but notice your efforts.

I look for people with a high energy level and a great attitude, people with a 'see what needs to be done and get it done' mentality. I want employees who are willing to step beyond their traditional job and do whatever needs to be done, whether it's taking out the trash or answering the phone if the receptionist is busy. Those attributes indicate a true professional and are definitely plusses on my superstar checklist.

In fact, I once hired an employee who had no experience at all in the staffing industry. What she did have, in addition to the basic skills I needed, was a positive professional attitude and a desire to work. I've never regretted

that decision because she proved herself a valuable member of the team who lived up to the professionalism she showed up front.

Step 5: Respect

Respect and professionalism go hand-in-hand. It's not really possible to be professional if you aren't also respectful of your employer and coworkers, and of yourself.

A superstar employee respects and upholds the company's core values. As a representative of the company, you must reflect these values in everything you do. From your attire to your attitude, there are so many ways of showing respect for the workplace.

Time is of the essence in most businesses; the way you use your time can indicate either respect or its lack. Getting to work on time, observing the time limits for lunch and breaks, working until the end of your shift—these habits show that you respect your employer by working efficiently when you are expected to be on duty.

Holding up your part of the team's responsibilities also shows that you respect the work and your colleagues. Carrying your weight is one of the surest signs that you respect everyone's contribution to the effort.

Perhaps one of the hallmarks of superstardom is the acknowledgment that no one is perfect. If your boss speaks to you about a performance issue, maintain a respectful attitude. Even if you hadn't realized that the problem existed, listen—and respond—respectfully. You can always ask for clarification, even after the discussion is over. What you can't do is take back anything disrespectful or negative that you might say.

In work, just like life, showing respect earns respect. You can't go wrong by making this part of your professional package.

Step 6: Ownership

An employee's willingness to take ownership of all that he or she does speaks volumes to his or her employer. This goes beyond accountability, because ownership means expanding outside yourself and becoming

invested in the company and its success.

You can do this by recognizing that your work performance is not based on the hours clocked in, but on the productivity you deliver during those hours. Filling a space for eight hours a day while you do the bare minimum of work is not the mark of a superstar. Doing the job that is expected of you to the absolute best of your ability is.

Show that you care about the company by carefully evaluating your own work and determining if there are ways in which you can be even more efficient. Look back at your job description from time to time to be sure you're hitting all the marks; don't wait for your boss to tell you that you're missing a step or doing something incorrectly.

A superstar recognizes that he or she is part of a team, and makes a conscious effort to ensure that the team shines as a whole. If you see an area where the team can function more effectively, speak up. Share your idea with your supervisor, who will appreciate the fact that you're clearly invested in the company's success.

Seeking additional training is a great way to take ownership. Taking an interest in advancing your professional development shows your employer that you are committed to the profession and to growing within the company. It helps your employer to know that the investment he or she made in hiring you was profitable.

Test Your Pro Skills

Consider the following scenarios that involved my staffing company and the way a true pro employee would handle each one:

1. All applicants are required to submit applications online rather than in person. When a person walks in to apply, the receptionist says, "We take applications only online; walk-in interviews are not permitted."

Does that sound like a superstar response? No. A superstar would say: "Thank you for coming in. We do interviews only by appointment, but since you have come in, I will gladly scan a copy of your resume. If you would like to use one of our computers, you can complete the online application, and I can attach your résumé to your file. I can also look on our recruiter's calendar to see when she has a space open for an interview,and we can go ahead and schedule you."

2. Applicants may have to wait a few minutes for their scheduled interviews. The receptionist curtly asks for a copy of their license and then returns to her work while the applicants sit in silence.

A superstar would greet each applicant with positive and cheerful energy to make a great first impression. The receptionist should stop whatever she is doing to respectfully welcome the applicant, offer a drink of water, and ask if she can be of assistance in any way.

3. It's a busy office, and the phone rings every few minutes, often interrupting the receptionist's other work. Would you grab the phone and simply say: "Part-Time Pros," and then wait for the caller to speak?

Not if you're a superstar. It's much better to answer with a positive, upbeat tone. It will make a much better impression on the caller to hear: "Thank you for calling Part-Time Pros; how may I help you?"

Becoming a superstar is a goal you should strive to achieve. Make a commitment to Be a Pro—be aware of Balance, Efficiency, Accountability, Professionalism, Respect, and Ownership. These qualities add up to a superstar employee; keep them at the forefront, and your employer can't help but notice.

SECTION 3

Understanding an Employer's Needs

Small business owners are busy people. When they have a job opening, they not only need to fill a vacant position but they also have to take time away from their own work to review applications and interview prospects. Small business owners do not want or need to waste time with an applicant who isn't serious. So, if you are not serious about a job, or if you know going into an interview that you're going to turn down the job if it's offered, don't waste the employer's time. It's disrespectful and unprofessional, and should you ever apply there again, you probably won't be considered.

When you are hired for a job, you want your employer to understand that your job is just one of the many priorities in your own life. You want him or her to understand when you need a day off, or have to come in late, or need to leave early to take care of personal business. However, this is two-way street. One of the things that truly professional employees know is that it's not all about them.

If you expect your employer to understand and meet your needs, you must understand and meet his or her needs, at least as they pertain to you

as an employee. Your employer is a person, too, with a family, a home, financial concerns, a personal life, and problems. What he or she needs from you as an employee is to understand his or her needs from a business perspective. The basic essential need of an employer is to have employees who are dependable, invested, empathetic, and engaged.

Be dependable

The number one thing any employer needs from you is dependability. You know what's expected of you in general terms—get to work on time, complete your tasks efficiently and effectively. However, dependability goes beyond these things if you really want to shine. To be an employee your boss can depend on, be true to your word. If you say you will do something or be somewhere at a specific time, deliver on it. Don't make the boss have to come looking for what he or she has every right to expect to receive.

Business owners and managers don't want to micromanage, but that's what they're forced to do if they've had the bad experience of hiring employees who aren't dependable. If you truly deliver on what your employer needs, the management experience will be so much better on both sides. Your boss will be confident that you are dependable and won't have to look over your shoulder, and you will have the fulfillment of knowing that your employer trusts you.

Be invested

Employers want to know that their employees are willing and eager to learn new skills and take on new assignments to improve the company's overall performance. You can show your investment in the company by asking questions and trying to come up with solutions to problems or more efficient ways to complete tasks. This also adds to your level of dependability, because it lets management know that you are alert, aware, and on top of what's going on. It shows a commitment to the organization's success, which is high on every employer's list of needs.

Another way to show your investment is to be respectful of the

company's time. Your employer should want to have a relationship with you and should be concerned about you as a person. If you have a family situation or personal problem, it's fine to let your boss know about it, but without any drama. Your employer will appreciate being advised of what's going on, particularly if the situation might require you to take some time off. Just be sure to keep your conversations professional, without getting emotional or dramatic and involving the entire staff in your story.

Be empathetic

Bosses are people, too. Just as you have to balance your work and home life, so does your boss. Your employer could very well have personal problems that you are unaware of, and it might be difficult for a manager to share personal details with staff. If you sense that something is wrong, be empathetic and ask if he or she is okay. Offer to help if you can. If your employer does share personal details, be professional and respect his or her privacy. Don't make your manager's home life fodder for the office grapevine.

Empathy doesn't apply only to bad situations. You know the feeling of satisfaction you experience when your employer praises you for a job very well done? That feeling goes both ways. If your employer has implemented a new system that streamlines the workflow or figured out a solution to a thorny problem, there's absolutely nothing wrong with expressing your appreciation. Managers need feedback as much as employees do. I certainly feel energized and motivated when my staff acknowledges something I've done that has improved things in the office.

Be engaged

For many small business owners, running a company depends largely on numbers. Not just the bottom line that indicates profit but reports and surveys that indicate which employees are engaged in actively working toward the company's growth and success.

I recently read the results of a survey in which 40 percent of respondents indicated that they were disengaged at work. Nearly half of the people

surveyed admitted that they go to work for the paycheck and nothing more. They have not made any personal investment in their job or the company. What these people might not realize is that their employers are likely to have read the same survey. When the time comes to lay off staff, those who do the bare minimum will be the first to go.

If you are new to the workforce, you can tell if you have what it takes to be an engaged, dependable employee by assessing your approach to your education. Did you float through school, getting passing grades but not working very hard? Or did you strive to get the best grades you possibly could, challenging yourself by taking courses that stretched your abilities and taught you more than what was covered in textbooks? If you're already a proven striver and achiever, you'll bring those same qualities to work with you, to the delight of the person who hires you. If you weren't engaged in school, you probably won't be engaged at work, though this is something you can certainly change.

Your work ethic is as important as your résumé. You may look great on paper, but if your commitment and engagement are lacking, your work ethic will show in the way you approach your job, and nothing can compensate for a lackluster attitude or sloppy work ethic. It really is that important to your employer that you demonstrate the willingness to gain the skills you need and work hard at the job you've been hired to do.

Become engaged—in your own specific job, in the work of your team, in the company as a whole. You may be surprised how much more you enjoy going to work when you branch outside your own cubicle and become involved in the bigger picture. Trust me, your employer will notice.

You want to be the kind of employee your employer would hate to lose. That's what managers want. When I hire someone, I'm looking for a person who will want to stay with the company for years, someone I want to see grow within the company.

Be in it for the long haul

If you bounce around from one job to another, staying a year here or eighteen months there, it's not going to bode well for you. Employers want

to hire individuals who are accountable for their actions, who understand that unprofessional or disrespectful behavior will eventually have a negative impact. For example, my company won't consider an applicant who has held three or more jobs for a year or less, because this indicates a lack of commitment to an employer. If you were laid off (which does not question your commitment) from 3 employers in a row, it does cause concern with your performance. The reputation of Part-Time Pros depends on my staff recommending only the highest qualified applicants to our clients, since we are the gatekeepers who weed out the applicants. Therefore, we have to follow strict policies and guidelines, and applicants must understand that their prior employment decisions will affect their future prospects.

Of course, there are many valid reasons for changing jobs, but before you leave a position, be sure you are making the right decision, one you can support later in an interview with a prospective employer.

A Word to Recent Graduates

Students who have recently graduated often find themselves in a difficult situation, applying for jobs for which they feel qualified but considered only for those that they see as entry level. It's a conundrum—you're not qualified because you don't have enough experience, but no one will hire you to give you the experience you need.

My advice is to reevaluate your needs and perceptions. A recent graduate, who interviewed with my company after having submitted many résumés on her own, stated that she wanted an annual salary of $45,000. Lisa, my recruiter, knows the market well and told the young woman that she honestly did not think she would be able to place her for that salary. The girl was surprised, and said that no one had told her that before. When Lisa explained that she would find more success looking for jobs in the high $20,000 to low $30,000 range, the applicant agreed to adjust her search.

The following week we sent her for an interview as a receptionist with a company that generally hires above the grade, meaning that they look for highly skilled employees they can later promote. The young woman took the job at a starting salary of $34,000, and four months later was offered a

promotion to the marketing department, her goal all along.

It's important for graduates to understand that the jobs are out there, but you can't have an overblown sense of your own worth or start out looking for a promotion before you're even hired. We all have to start somewhere, and you'll have a much more fruitful job search if you are realistic about where your skills and experience fit into the current market. Yes, you've worked hard and earned your degree, but it doesn't automatically entitle you to the job of your dreams. In the scenario I just described, the young woman essentially promoted herself through hard work. In her case, the promotion was truly earned because she focused on the job she was hired to do, exceeding her employer's expectations, and her employer recognized her potential.

I've talked in earlier chapters about the need to be honest with yourself regarding your abilities and needs before you start your job search. Honesty remains one of the things that employers want to see in potential hires, because it indicates professionalism and maturity. I know this because I speak from experience.

When I graduated from college, with a double major and very good grades, I basically thought I knew it all. Of course I'd find a great job based on my wonderful credentials. I sent out resumes and was contacted personally by a successful local banker who was an acquaintance of my father. Clearly, my ship had come in. This man owned many businesses, and if he'd called me personally, he must have wanted to hire me.

When I returned his call and he asked what I wanted to do, I replied, "I can do whatever." When he then asked about my goals and strengths, and exactly what I was interested in doing, I couldn't answer the question. He told me to get in touch with him when I figured it out. Ouch. Here I'd basically had a job offer handed to me on a silver platter, and I'd thrown a stick of dynamite right onto it and blew it up. All because I'd felt entitled to a job and hadn't taken the time to consider what I really wanted to—and could—do. It was a hard lesson to learn, but I've never forgotten it.

So, in addition to the fact that you are well educated, you must answer two essential questions before you start interviewing: What do you want to do? What will a company gain by hiring you?

The Bottom Line

Although the basic responsibilities of a company are to manage effectively, hire the right people, and track performance, the employer's basic need is for the employees to work hard and perform well.

It is up to you, as an employee, to understand that if the company is not successful, you are out of a job. Companies are made successful by the combined efforts of all employees, from the receptionist to the owners and every person on the payroll. Nothing short of a dedicated effort on everyone's part will lead to success. When you understand this, you will truly comprehend your employer's needs and be willing to give your maximum effort to the cause.

SECTION 4

How to Handle a Performance Issue

Managers all have their own style. Some may discuss a performance issue with an employee immediately, some may take time to think about their approach, and some may wait until an official performance appraisal to bring up the issue. I hope your manager's style is one of the first two.

Preventing performance issues

Like needs and expectations, a performance issue is a topic that goes both ways between employers and employees. One of the biggest reasons performance issues arise is poor communication. If you feel uncertain about what is expected of you, take steps to ensure that you are fulfilling your required duties.

- Read your job description to reestablish what is expected and whether you are meeting those responsibilities. If anything is unclear, ask your supervisor to help define what the description calls for.

- If you do not have a job description, write your own. This is an acceptable, proactive approach that your employer should appreciate. During your first month of employment, when you've become comfortable with the position, write out everything that you do. Don't worry about format; just get your duties down on paper. Bring the list to your manager and ask for a conversation to clarify what's expected. Explain that what you've written is what you feel is expected; ask if anything is missing and express that you want to be clear about those expectations to be sure you meet them.

- Communicate with your employer when you need backup or support. If you feel overwhelmed or realize that you don't have the necessary training for what's expected, address this right away. Tell your supervisor that you would like to be trained to do the job correctly and efficiently, rather than try to figure it out and waste time. Should you need help with a deadline, it's better to tell your manager than either miss the deadline or submit shoddy work, both of which would make the boss think you can't meet his or her expectations.

Responding to an employer's concerns

Every employee is bound to need a bit of constructive criticism on occasion; it's part of how you learn exactly what's expected of you. The way in which your employer approaches this may certainly be a factor in how you respond, but regardless of his or her style, you must always maintain a professional demeanor.

An employee's reaction and response to criticism, complaints, or concerns from management are big indicators of his or her level of professionalism. Even if you disagree with what's being said, do not be defensive or argumentative. Let your manager say what he or she needs to say without interruption and then state your case calmly and evenly.

It's an unavoidable fact that not every employer and employee will get along well. Your manager might have a style or approach you don't care for, but it's important to maintain your professionalism and acknowledge that

you two just are not alike. If your boss's style is different from what you are accustomed to, you have to be aware of that and keep your responses professional regardless of how it makes you feel. In short, adapting to a different personality will help resolve issues much more quickly than confrontation will.

No one likes being called on the carpet, even if it's done gently. If you feel too emotional or overwhelmed to make your case then and there, tell your employer that you'd like some time to think about what he or she has said and ask if you can meet again in 24 or 48 hours to discuss it. Take that time to write down your thoughts and responses, and let your emotions diffuse so that you can address the matter calmly.

Not long ago I had to address a performance issue after noticing on a few occasions that our office manager was not meeting all of our expectations. Based on my observations, I made notes about the issues, which included the following:

- Not conversing with applicants who were waiting for appointments.
- Using an inappropriate tone of voice and shortness on the phone.

I wrote up my concerns and called the office manager in for a meeting in which I discussed each issue as it related to the expectations put forward in her job description, and explained how her current performance was not meeting those expectations. We had an open discussion about how to improve her performance, including what she needed to do and what steps we could take to help her meet her goals.

The meeting was not at all confrontational, since it was not my intention to reprimand or scold her but rather to show her where her performance had begun to slip.

Because it was important for me to understand any underlying reasons for the change, I gave her the opportunity to address each issue in turn. Afterward, I wrote a summary of the meeting that we signed, and she wrote her own document detailing her feelings and reactions to our conversation. Both documents are now part of her employee file.

Here is an example of the positive and proactive approach from employer and employee perspectives:

Employer's issue:

The lack of conversation while someone is waiting for his or her interview.

[Employee] is the first impression of Part-Time Pros. Just as she gives applicants a first impression score, they give her and us a first impression score. The energy level needs to be high, positive, and cheerful. Life can be stressful and exhausting, but it is up to us to make a fabulous first impression. Every applicant should be greeted with a smile, a nice greeting, and an offer to get some water or be of service, not "I need a copy of your license." Activity should be paused to greet someone.

[Employee] recognized this and will make a more conscious effort to be more friendly and outgoing to applicants.

Tone of voice and shortness on the phone.

There have been instances where we have witnessed [Employee] answering the phone and sounding as if she would rather be anywhere but there and that she is irritated by having to answer the phone. All calls should be answered with a cheerful, upbeat, and happy tone.

[Employee] and I talked about now answering the phone with the following: "Thank you for calling Part-Time and Tulsa-Med Pros, how may I help you?" instead of "Part-Time Pros and Tulsa-Med Pros."

Employee's response:

In our meeting regarding my performance, I honestly felt comfortable.I know that you appreciate my work and me. Having the ability to come to you with concerns about the office or personal issues that affect me daily makes working here that much more enjoyable.

In the meeting, we went over some issues where you felt that I was not meeting your expectations. While it may not be enjoyable being told you are doing something wrong or badly, I appreciated having my attitude addressed.

Sometimes I find myself jaded by the day-to-day dealings with candidates and their repetitive questions, and I can dwell on that. Having someone address this issue in a nice manner pushes me to do better. Also, knowing that you do support me and want me to do the best I can helped the overall morale of the meeting. Having the open dialogue and being able to explain my side of the story also made the meeting feel more motivational than disciplinary.

After the meeting, receiving the form about what was discussed was a good way to review and know what is expected from me in the future. Also knowing that it would impact future growth let me know that, for advancement, you wanted to see that I could take the direction and apply it to my work.

Overall, I left the meeting knowing that I needed to make changes, and which changes you wanted me to make. It made me step back and realize that every time I am asked the same question, it is that person's first time asking that question. I was reminded that I needed to put myself in the applicants' shoes and know that the question is not being asked to drive me nuts, but because they need to know how the system works.

I appreciated receiving this document. It showed me that my employee was sincere about her desire to improve her performance, and reinforced that we were both on the same page.

If your employer calls you in for a performance issue, you should be given a written summary of the meeting. If one is not offered, ask for it, and then use it to draft your own response and reaction to the meeting. This will show your manager that you have taken the issue seriously. As in any discussion about performance, be professional, even if you are expressing disagreement with any of your employer's points.

The sensitive issue of promotions

Consider this scenario. You have learned that a position is about to open in the department you've always wanted to work in. The position is a higher grade than your current job, with more responsibility and a higher salary. You just know you're qualified, and you've worked for the company for two years, so you express interest and wait for the call. But you don't get the job. Your reaction is to:

- Openly complain that the person chosen for the job isn't qualified.

- Refuse to talk to the person who got the job.

- Throw a tantrum like a two-year-old because you didn't get what you wanted.

- Act professionally and maturely and learn from the experience.

Okay, this one's a given, but although it's undeniably disappointing, even this painful experience can be turned into a valuable lesson. First, it's a mistake for an employee to assume he or she will be promoted simply by virtue of longevity. Just as when someone is first hired, an employer has many factors to weigh when choosing someone for a promotion. The fact that a particular employee is not chosen isn't a negative reflection on him or her; the employee simply was not the best choice to fulfill the employer's needs at the time.

If you are denied a promotion, ask to speak with your manager privately. Ask why you were not selected for the position, and accept the response calmly. Explain that you would like to grow into the new position and ask for advice about the skills you need to acquire to make that possible. Just as you had to clarify your goals when you started your job search, you must do the same again so your employer can offer the best guidance.

A formal performance evaluation can be a good time for this discussion. However, if no evaluation is planned for the near future, it's acceptable to request a meeting to talk with your employer about your goals. Again, this proactive step shows your commitment to your own professional growth and the company's success. In closing, I would encourage you to BE A PRO. Know that you are an investment that the company has made and do your part to control the ROI!

Index

Top "Ten" Lists – not all of these lists contain ten bullet points, but you get the idea.